'HOW TO'

BOOK OF
VEGETABLE
GARDENING

ANN BONAR

BROCKHAMPTON PRESS

The **'HOW TO'** Book of Vegetable Gardening
explains in straightforward terms – through the
use of concise texts, charts, photographs, and
diagrams; the principles and techniques that
will enable you to gain more produce, and
more enjoyment, from your vegetable garden.

'HOW TO'

Contents

The 'How To' Book of Vegetable Gardening
was conceived, edited and designed by
Simon Jennings and Company Limited

This edition published 1996 by
Brockhampton Press Ltd,
20 Bloomsbury Street,
London WC1B 3QA

Text and illustrations
© 1981 Simon Jennings & Co Ltd

ISBN 1 86019 219 X

Printed and bound in U.A.E.

THE AUTHOR

Ann Bonar is usually described as a horticultural journalist – a label which tends to obscure the facts that she is both an experienced horticulturist and a successful writer. She has many years experience of commercial fruit growing, and has regularly contributed to a number of magazines and journals on gardening topics. This exhausting schedule has been combined with lecturing, editing and the writing of several books.

Introduction

Growing your own vegetables is easy to do even if you don't know much about it. Most of them are grown from seed, which is sown in mid spring; once the seed has sprouted, practically all that has to be done is to keep each crop clear of weeds, and supplied with water and food.

In a few weeks or months, it will be ready for harvesting, to be eaten at once, or stored for winter use. A few vegetables are grown from plants or tubers, e.g. asparagus, potatoes – they are also planted in spring.

It would be asking too much to expect all of them to be trouble-free, but there are more than enough for you to be able to provide your family with fresh, succulent vegetables all through the year, even at your first attempt.

Once you have tasted your own home-grown lettuces with their delicious nutty flavour and crisp leaves, and baby courgettes cut straight from the plant into the pot, your greengrocer will have lost a customer.

Not only that, your vegetables will contain very much greater quantities of vitamins than those left lying about for hours or days before being cooked. For instance, vitamin C and part of vitamin B are gradually destroyed by light.

Another great advantage of home-produced crops is that the cost is so much less than that of vegetables which have passed from grower, to wholesaler, to shop, and perhaps travelled several hundred miles in the process.

What it will cost you instead is your time, but there is a great deal of satisfaction to be had in being able to eat what you have actually grown.

5

Choosing and planning

When you are deciding what to grow, there is no point in choosing vegetables that you or your family don't like. Space will probably be at a premium, and each plant must give as high a yield as possible in proportion to its size, as well as being one which is popular.

The type of vegetable you are to grow is also important. Do you want everyday vegetables such as runner beans and cabbages? Do you want winter-hardy vegetables which will fill the 'Hungry Gap' from early to late spring: kale, sprouting broccoli or leeks? Or luxury crops such as asparagus and chicory?

If you have a warm garden, sheltered from wind, you will be able to grow the subtropical vegetables, such as peppers and aubergines, and you will be able to harvest the hardy crops earlier or later than usual.

Use of space
With a little planning, the vegetable garden will not only yield maximum produce, but it will also look good.

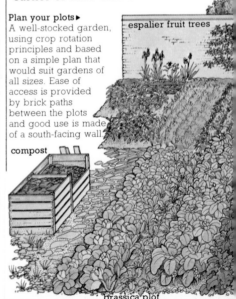

Plan your plots ▶
A well-stocked garden, using crop rotation principles and based on a simple plan that would suit gardens of all sizes. Ease of access is provided by brick paths between the plots and good use is made of a south-facing wall.

espalier fruit trees

compost

brassica plot

The soil of your garden will further affect your choice; heavy clay types favour lettuce, the cabbage family and runner beans. Sandy soils are best for most root crops – carrots, beetroot and so on.

The part of the garden where you grow the crops should be sunny. Very few vegetables can be grown in shady areas. It should not be a frost pocket, and should have soil which does not hold water. A water supply within easy reach, and a garden shed nearby, will ensure that fetching and carrying is kept to a minimum.

Once you have made your selection, you should then plan the sequence of vegetables, depending on the time each crop takes to mature and to which rotation group it belongs.

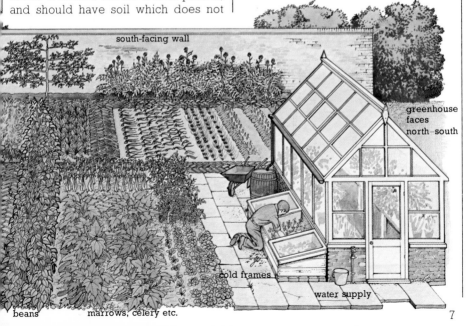

south-facing wall

greenhouse faces north–south

cold frames

water supply

beans   marrows, celery etc.

Crop rotation

Vegetable crop rotation is very important. Generally, three groups of vegetables are grown in turn, one each year, on a given piece of ground. This results in the maximum use of the plant foods in the soil, and prevents soil and plant pests and fungus diseases accumulating.

For example, *Group A* vegetables could consist of any of the beans, peas, spinach, celery, lettuce, etc. They all need good dressings of rotted garden compost or manure during the winter or spring before planting.

Group B could include the cabbage family, turnip and radish, etc., and would follow Group A on the same ground in the second season. *Group C*: most of the root vegetables, potatoes and fruiting vegetables (aubergine, sweetcorn) – would take the place of Group B in the third season, to be followed by Group A in the fourth year.

Each of these groups contain veget-

●Group A
Grow peas, beans, celery, spinach etc., in the first year.
See pages 10 and 11

●Group B
First year crops would be the cabbage family, radishes and turnips. *See pages 14 and 15*

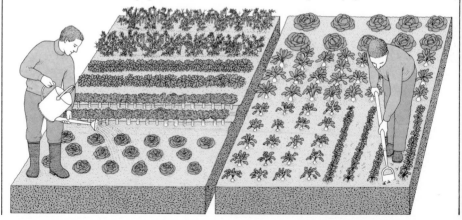

ables whose roots reach to different depths, and so use different plant foods. The cabbage family is very likely to contract root fungus diseases from the soil, e.g. clubroot, and pests such as cabbage root fly, but these can be avoided by growing on the same piece of ground only once in three years.

Group C vegetables like the mineral plant food potassium in the soil, so a potash-containing fertilizer would be needed when preparing the soil.

Group B vegetables need the plant food nitrogen to develop well-coloured, strong leafy growth, and will get a good deal of it as a result of the activities of the pea and bean roots in the season before.

There is also a fourth, smaller group. The crops here are outside the rotation, because they are either permanent or can be grown again in the same place without harm. It includes asparagus and onions.

●**Group C**
Root crops, sweetcorn, peppers and aubergines on a well prepared soil. *See pages 18 and 19*

●**Outside the rotation**
Grow onions, garlic, asparagus etc., on the same soil year after year. *See pages 22 and 23*

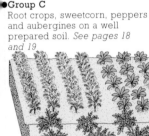

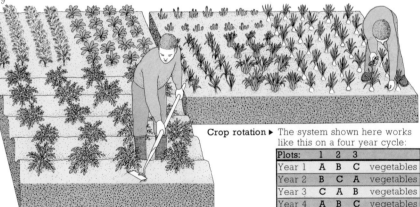

Crop rotation ▶ The system shown here works like this on a four year cycle:

Plots:	1	2	3	
Year 1	A	B	C	vegetables
Year 2	B	C	A	vegetables
Year 3	C	A	B	vegetables
Year 4	A	B	C	vegetables

9

Plot one vegetables

In Plot 1 in the first year you can grow the vegetables in Group A. They are all vegetables which grow best in moist, heavy soil, which has had rotted farm manure, garden compost or a similar kind of rotted organic matter dug into it some weeks, or even months, before the vegetables are planted or sown.

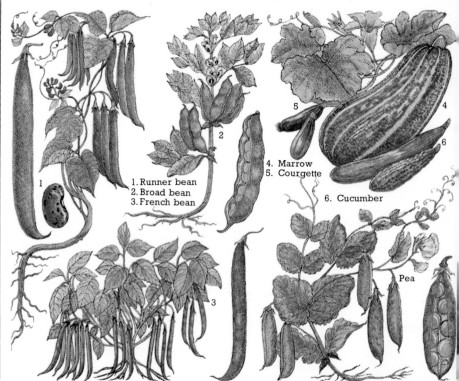

1. Runner bean
2. Broad bean
3. French bean
4. Marrow
5. Courgette
6. Cucumber
Pea

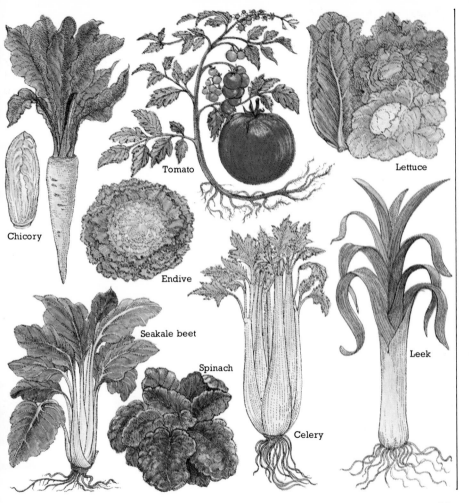

Chicory

Tomato

Lettuce

Endive

Seakale beet

Spinach

Celery

Leek

11

Vegetable	Nutrition Vitamins/Minerals	Yield Per 30cm/1ft	Time to mature from sowing
Broad Bean	High vitamin C Some B High protein	$\frac{1}{4}$–$\frac{1}{2}$kg ($\frac{1}{2}$–1lb)	14 weeks
French Bean	Some B Low protein	$\frac{1}{4}$–$\frac{1}{2}$kg ($\frac{1}{2}$–1lb)	10–12 weeks
Haricots	Some B Low protein	30g (1oz)	16–18 weeks
Runner Bean	Some calcium	1$\frac{1}{2}$kg (3lb)	14 weeks
Chicory	Some A and B	1–2 plants	26–29 weeks *To lifting (before forcing)*
Celery	Trace vitamins Some minerals	1–2 plants	18 weeks **Self Blanching** 28 weeks **Winter**
Cucumber ridge	Mostly water Trace vitamins	12–15 per plant	12 weeks
Cucumber indoor	Mostly water Trace vitamins	20–30 per plant	10–12 weeks

Vegetable	Nutrition Vitamins/Minerals	Yield Per 30cm/1ft	Time to mature from sowing
Endive	Some A and B	1 plant	12 weeks
Leek	Some A	2 plants	30–45 weeks
Lettuce	Some A, B, C, E	1–2 plants	8–14 weeks **Summer** 26 weeks **Winter**
Marrow	Mostly water	5–6 per plant	12–14 weeks
Courgette	Mostly water	15–20 per plant	10–12 weeks
Pea	Some A, B, C High protein	$\frac{1}{4}$–$\frac{1}{2}$kg ($\frac{1}{2}$–1lb)	11–14 weeks *Depending on variety*
Seakale Beet	Some A, B and K	$\frac{1}{4}$kg ($\frac{1}{2}$lb)	16 weeks
Spinach *including Perpetual Spinach*	High A, B and C High protein Iron	**Summer** 140g(5oz) **Winter** $\frac{1}{4}$kg($\frac{1}{2}$lb)	6–8 weeks
Tomatoes	Some A, B and C Low protein	**Outdoors** 2–3kg(4–6lb)	18 weeks

Plot two vegetables

Plot 2 in the first year will be used for growing the cabbage family and other vegetables needing the same manurial treatment. This can consist of applying rotted organic matter in late autumn, but no later. Alternatively, you need not apply any, if the soil is in good condition, as the plant's roots will make use of the fertility from the previous application, and the nitrogen supplied as a result of the activity of the pea and bean roots.

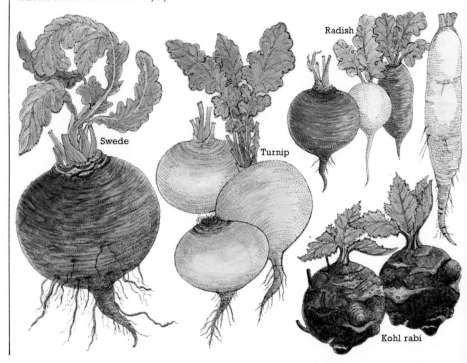

Swede

Turnip

Radish

Kohl rabi

14

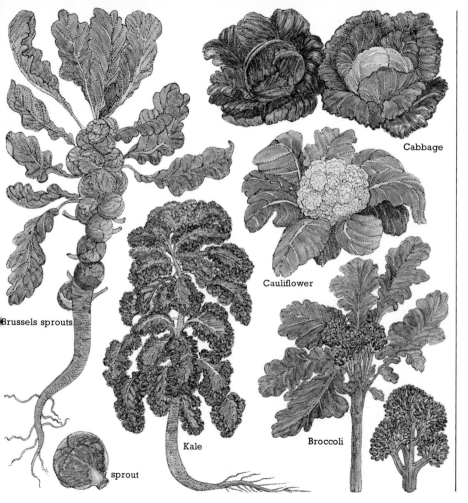

Cabbage

Cauliflower

Brussels sprouts

Kale

sprout

Broccoli

15

Nutrition and yield/Plot two

Vegetable	Nutrition Vitamins/Minerals	Yield Per 30cm/1ft	Time to mature from sowing
Broccoli Sprouting	Some A and B Medium protein	$\frac{1}{2}$kg(1lb) per plant	40 weeks
Brussels Sprouts	Some A and B Medium protein	1kg(2lb) per plant	28–36 weeks
Cabbage	Some A and B High C Low protein	**Red** & **Autumn** 1–1$\frac{1}{2}$kg(2–3lb) **Savoys** & **Winter** 1–1$\frac{1}{4}$kg(2–2$\frac{1}{2}$lb) **Spring** $\frac{3}{4}$kg(1$\frac{1}{2}$lb)	20–25 weeks 28–32 weeks 40–44 weeks
Cauliflower	Some A and B High C Medium protein	1–2 plants $\frac{1}{2}$–1kg(1–2lb)	**Summer** 8–24 weeks **Winter** 36–38 weeks
Kale	High A and C Some B	$\frac{3}{4}$kg(1$\frac{1}{2}$lb)	36–52 weeks
Kohl Rabi	Some minerals	56–112g(2–4oz)	8–10 weeks
Radish	Some A, B, C Low protein	**Summer** $\frac{1}{2}$kg(1lb) **Winter** $\frac{1}{2}$kg(1lb)	3–6 weeks 20 weeks

Vegetable	Nutrition Vitamins/Minerals	Yield Per 30cm/1ft	Time to mature from sowing
Swede	Some A and B High C	$\frac{1}{4}-\frac{1}{2}$kg(1–2lb)	20–24 weeks
Turnip	Trace B6 Low minerals	**Maincrop** $\frac{1}{2}-\frac{1}{4}$kg($\frac{1}{2}$–1lb) **Early** 168g(6oz)	10–12 weeks 6–8 weeks

BRUSSELS SPROUTS

Brussels sprouts are among the hardiest of vegetables and, with careful handling, can provide fresh produce in the depths of winter. They tend to be affected by the same pests as other brassicas, but they are especially prone to attacks from birds – no doubt due to the shortage of winter food. The top leaves make an excellent vegetable dish, so there is very little wastage with sprouts. *See page 52*

Removing leaves
In autumn, the lower leaves will turn yellow and can be removed. When the lower sprouts have begun to swell, take out the tops to encourage the remainder.

Harvesting sprouts
Always pick the bottom sprouts first. Take just a few from each plant at each picking. A good plant will have closely packed "buttons" all the way up the stem

17

Plot three vegetables

Next to Plot 2 in the first year is the third group of vegetables in the rotation – Group C. Here will be most of the root vegetables, including the tubers, potatoes and Jerusalem artichokes, and some of the fruiting vegetables such as aubergines and sweet peppers. These are crops which need potassium but no recently applied organic matter, so they should be grown in soil which was manured before the previous crop. The fertilizer sulphate of potash, or wood-ash (from bonfires), should be forked into the ground a week or so before sowing or planting.

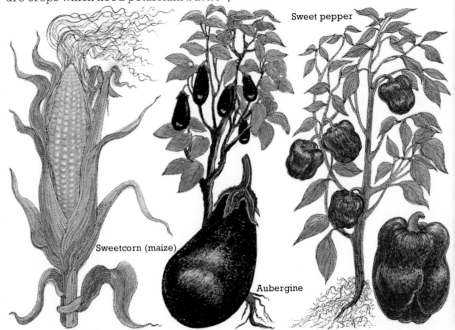

Sweet pepper

Sweetcorn (maize)

Aubergine

18

Celeriac

Beetroot

Parsnip

Carrot

Potato

Jerusalem artichoke

Nutrition and yield/Plot three

Vegetable	Nutrition Vitamins/Minerals	Yield Per 30cm/1ft	Time to mature from sowing
Aubergine	Some minerals Low carbohydrates	1 plant per 75cm(2½ft) 4 fruits per plant	18 weeks
Beetroot	Some B and C Low protein	**Summer** 3 plants 84g(3oz) per plant **Winter** 2 plants 224g(8oz) per plant	8–10 weeks 19 weeks
Carrot	Very high A Some B, C, E Low protein	**Maincrop** 140g(5oz) per plant 3 plants **Early crop & salad** 6 plants 42g(1½oz) per plant	14–18 weeks 10–12 weeks
Celeriac	Some minerals	¼–½kg (½–1lb) per plant	26–30 weeks
Jerusalem Artichoke	Some minerals potassium	½–¾kg (1–1½lb) per plant	36 weeks

Vegetable	Nutrition Vitamins/Minerals	Yield Per 30cm/1ft	Time to mature from sowing
Parsnip	Low carbohydrate	$\frac{1}{2}$–$\frac{3}{4}$kg (1–1$\frac{1}{2}$lb) per plant	32 weeks
Pepper Sweet	Very high C	$\frac{1}{2}$–1kg (1–1$\frac{1}{2}$lb) per plant	32 weeks
Potato	Some B and C High protein	**Maincrop** $\frac{3}{4}$–1kg (1–1$\frac{1}{2}$lb) **Early crop** $\frac{1}{2}$kg (1lb) per plant	20–22 weeks 13 weeks
Sweetcorn	Mainly carbohydrate	2 cobs (Ears) per plant	14 weeks

STORING CARROTS

For an effective method of storing carrots through the winter, stack them in a conical shape with the roots pointing inwards. Cover the stack with clean, dry straw and complete the structure with a layer of fine soil. Make a few air holes when the soil has consolidated.

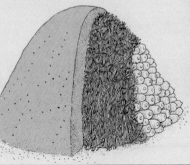

Preparation
Before stacking, cut off the foliage, shake off loose soil, and check for disease.

Outside the rotation

The remaining vegetables are outside the rotation. Some are perennial and stay in their places for several years, once a satisfactory position has been found for them. This applies to the onion family: onions, shallots, garlic. However, if one year a crop has rotting at the base of the bulbs, the next season's crop should be grown in a different place.

Nutrition and yield

Vegetable	Nutrition Vitamins/Minerals	Yield Per 30cm/1ft	Time to mature from sowing
Asparagus	Trace C Low mineral content	20 spears per plant	**From sowing** 3 years **From planting** 2 years
Garlic	Mainly bactericide	2 bulbs	**Summer planting** 36 weeks **Other planting** 28 weeks
Globe Artichoke	Low mineral content	5 heads per plant 1 plant per metre (3ft)	**From sowing** 3 years **From planting** 2 years
Onion	Trace minerals content	**Maincrop** 336g(¾lb) **Spring onion** 112g(4oz) **Autumn sown** 224g(½lb)	18–22 weeks 6–9 weeks 40 weeks
Shallot	Trace mineral content	168g(6oz)	18–20 weeks

Globe artichoke

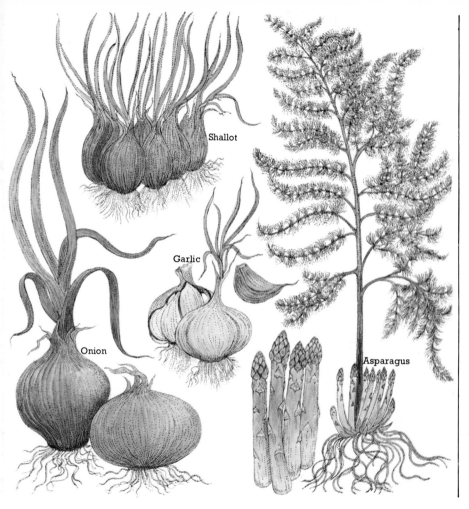

Shallot

Garlic

Onion

Asparagus

23

Gardening tools

GENERAL TOOLS

In addition to the cultivation tools shown opposite, you will find it necessary to have access to the equipment illustrated here.

Wheelbarrow
The universal modern wheelbarrow has a steel frame and body. Avoid impractical looking fibreglass types.

Watering can
You may manage without a hose but not without a watering can. Look for galvanised metal with a copper rose.

Tape, line and pins
A measuring tape is bound to be useful, and a garden line is essential for marking straight drills.

Gloves
Soft, pliable gloves are worn mainly for protection, but they can be very welcome during winter digging.

You will need fewer tools for successful vegetable gardening than for ornamental gardening, and your initial outlay need not be vast. Nevertheless, you should look for good quality equipment and not be tempted by exceptionally low prices. Gardening tools come in a very wide range of prices and an equally wide range of qualities. You want something that will last more than one season and cope with all the jobs you have in mind for it.

Always clean tools carefully after use and oil them during the winter. The oil inhibits rust formation. Metal shafted spades, rakes, hoes and forks are more durable than wooden ones but they are prone to rust and need more maintenance. Stainless steel varieties look very nice and they do not corrode, but they are very expensive and not necessarily any more effective than others. Make sure the handles of these implements are comfortable to use.

Spade
The first essential in any garden; turning the soil effectively is impossible without one.

Fork
The fork is the most versatile of garden tools: digging, spreading, lifting and turning are just some of its uses.

Dutch hoe
The most practical implement for weeding between rows.

Draw hoe
Useful for breaking-up soil and earthing-up.

Rake
The standard garden rake is vital in the preparation of a fine soil for sowing.

Onion hoe
For weeding below thick foliage.

Dibber
The best instrument for making planting holes.

Trowel
Used mainly in potting and transplanting work.

Hand fork
Ideal for lifting and separating young plants.

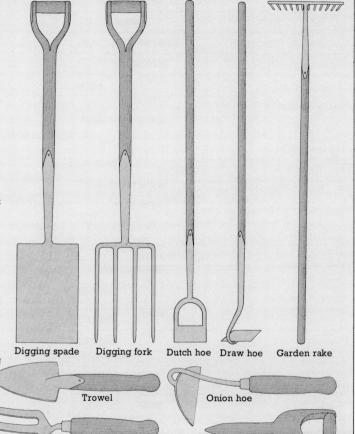

Digging spade Digging fork Dutch hoe Draw hoe Garden rake

Trowel

Onion hoe

Hand fork

Dibber

Gardener's calendar

	JAN	FEB	MAR	APR	MAY	JUN	JUL	AUG	SEP	OCT	NOV	DEC
Globe Artichoke												
Jerusalem Artichoke												
Asparagus												
Aubergine			•		•							
Broad Bean											•	
French Bean			•	•	•							
Runner Bean					•							
Beetroot												
Broccoli *sprouting*												
Brussels Sprouts												
Cabbage			•	•								
Carrot												
Cauliflower *summer*			•	•								
Cauliflower *winter*												
Celeriac			•		•							
Celery			•		•							
Chicory												
Water Cress	•	•						*winter*				•
Cucumber *indoor*												
Cucumber *ridge*				•	•							
Endive												

26

KEY Sow plant harvest store protect	JAN	FEB	MAR	APR	MAY	JUN	JUL	AUG	SEP	OCT	NOV	DEC
Garlic												
Kale												
Kohlrabi												
Leek												
Lettuce												
Onion												
Parsnip												
Pea												
Pepper												
Potato												
Radish												
Shallots												
Spinach					summer			winter				
Spinach Beet			Winter			summer					winter	
Seakale Beet												
Swede												
Sweetcorn												
Tomato outdoor												
Tomato indoor												
Turnip												
Vegetable Marrow												

Soil preparation

For the *Group A* vegetables the peas, beans, and others which are heavy feeders and need rich moist soil, rotted farm manure or garden compost should be mixed into the soil well in advance of planting or sowing.

For all but the runner beans, celery, cucumbers and marrows, the ground should be dug one spade deep in late autumn or early winter, mixing the manure both with the top soil and the bottom of the trench as you go. Application rate can be about 3kg per sq.m(7lb per sq.yd) for heavy soil, 4½kg(10lb) for average soil, and up to 7½kg (16lb) for sandy, gravelly or chalky soil.

Group B vegetables, which includes the cabbage family, kohlrabi, radish, swede and turnip, do not need manure to give the best results, provided they follow Group A on the same ground.

If the soil is too rich, or soft,cabbages and Brussels sprouts will be loose, not firm-hearted; cauliflowers will not be compact, the sprouting broccoli will produce leaves instead of florets, and the root crops will fork.

However, if no manure was given for the preceding group, some should be applied early in the autumn before the new growing season. This gives the soil a fairly long time to settle and become firm, and to absorb the organic matter. Digging to one spade's depth will do, but two will be better.

If the soil is acid, a lime dressing should be given several weeks after the application of manure. If it already contains chalk, is alkaline, or had lime given in the previous season, none should be given.

Group C vegetables, which follow the cabbage family group, do not need any winter treatment beyond the usual digging and clearing of weeds, rubbish and the remains of finished crops. No manure need be given.

However, these vegetables will need some fertilizer treatment. This should be mixed into the soil a week or ten days before sowing, if the crops are to mature where they are sown, or before planting, if transplanted or grown from tubers.

You can use sulphate of potash on its own: 14–28g per sq.m(½–1oz per sq.yd) is the rate of application. Mixing it with coarse sand makes it easier to put on evenly.

Ash from bonfires which consists mostly of burnt wood, is also good, and can be used at up to 224g per sq.m(8oz per sq.yd). Its potassium content is not very high, so it has to be given liberally.

A third possibility, if the soil is on the hungry side, is to use a compound fertilizer which contains nitrogen, phosphorus and potassium, the three most important mineral plant foods. This should contain only a little nitrogen, but a good deal of potassium.

The fourth section will need different treatments, according to which vegetable is to be grown.

Asparagus and globe artichokes are both heavy feeders, with a preference for a rich, moist, well-drained soil, so deep digging (two spades) with rotted organic matter mixed in to all levels, will be needed in winter, or early spring.

For onions, garlic and shallots, a moderate application of manure or garden compost should be dug in well in advance of planting or sowing. Sulphate of potash or wood-ash will be needed shortly before putting the seeds or sets in the ground.

If you are cultivating new ground, particularly soil which has been under grass, apply sulphate of potash and superphosphate in advance of sowing.

USING FERTILIZERS

General fertilisers
All plants will make demands on the soil for their food. Therefore, you should replace what they take out. All plants need nitrogen, potash and phosphorous – the three main constituents of general purpose fertilisers.

Using bonfire ash
Bonfire ash can be a good source of potash if the fire contained plenty of wood. Old wood, burned slowly, gives the best results and may be over 10% potash.

The vital fertilisers

NITROGEN	encourages good foliar growth and development
PHOSPHOROUS	good for root systems and quick-maturing plants
POTASSIUM	ensures balanced growth and strengthens plants

Pests and diseases

There are, potentially, a great many insect pests and diseases which can infest your crops. Each vegetable has a collection of possible troubles, some of which are specific to it and some of which will infect or nibble many others also.

Virus diseases are incurable, and easily confused with greenfly damage or mineral nutrient deficiency symptoms. If growth has ceased when these symptoms are present, you cannot see greenfly and know the soil to be fertile, suspect virus infection and destroy the plant.

In practice, however, you will find that it is the pests like caterpillars, greenfly and blackfly, slugs, birds and wireworms, and mildew or grey mould, which cause the most trouble most often. Some can occur on most crops; some can occur most years on a particular crop. But there are many ways of avoiding or preventing trouble so that you always get good harvests.

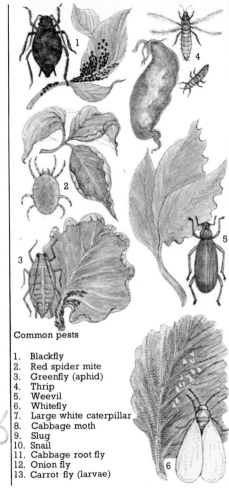

Common pests

1. Blackfly
2. Red spider mite
3. Greenfly (aphid)
4. Thrip
5. Weevil
6. Whitefly
7. Large white caterpillar
8. Cabbage moth
9. Slug
10. Snail
11. Cabbage root fly
12. Onion fly
13. Carrot fly (larvae)

Cut worm

Eel worm

Wire worm

RECOGNISING DISEASE

The 'plant' shown below is an amalgam of the more common diseases of vegetables – showing the usual symptoms.

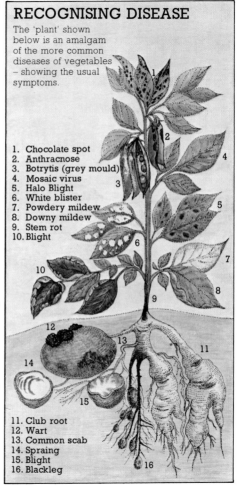

1. Chocolate spot
2. Anthracnose
3. Botrytis (grey mould)
4. Mosaic virus
5. Halo Blight
6. White blister
7. Powdery mildew
8. Downy mildew
9. Stem rot
10. Blight

11. Club root
12. Wart
13. Common scab
14. Spraing
15. Blight
16. Blackleg

Prevention and cure

One way of avoiding trouble will probably occur automatically, that is growing a mixture of crops; if only one crop is grown, even in a different place each year, epidemics of pests and diseases occur.

Rotating the vegetables, as already described, is another way, so that pests and diseases specific to certain crops do not accumulate in the soil.

Good cultivation is very important. By making sure that plants are never starved, thirsty or choked by weeds, and by daily watchfulness for the start of trouble, you may never need to spray with pesticides at all. You will have help too, from beneficial insects such as ladybirds and their larvae and from animals, such as hedgehogs and toads, which feed on some vegetable pests.

If, in spite of all your care, you begin to get infestations, you can often stop a pest or a disease getting a good grip on the plants by hand removal as soon as they are seen. Caterpillars, slugs and snails can be removed bodily; parts of plants like tips of shoots or young leaves with greenfly, blackfly or whitefly can be cut off.

As a precaution against further damage, you can then spray with a pesticide diluted with water. There are several proprietary kinds available now, which are both safe and effective to use, and which do no harm to beneficial insects.

Trouble	Appearance	Damage	Cure
Birds *pigeons sparrows blackbirds*	well known	peck holes in pea pods, cabbage family leaves, eat seeds, peck onion sets, tomato fruit, etc.	protect crops with netting
Blackfly	tiny black insects in clusters on tips of shoots and leaves	stunt new growth, decrease crops	remove with finger and thumb; spray bioresmethrin

Trouble	Appearance	Damage	Cure
Cabbage white butterfly caterpillars *cabbage family*	green and yellow with black spots, 2·5cm(1in) long	eat holes in leaves; 3–4 hatches a season	remove with finger and thumb; spray derris frequently
Cabbage root fly *cabbage family*	white maggots; adult fly 6mm(½in) long, like house fly	maggots eat roots which swell; plants die; seedlings and young plants mainly	put plastic foam disc on soil, round stems of plants, to prevent egg laying or treat soil·with bromophos
Carrot fly *celery, parsley, parsnip*	tiny white maggots; adult fly 8mm(⅜in) long	maggots tunnel into roots and feed; carrots rot	destroy infested roots; apply diazinon to soil before sowing
Club-root *cabbage family*	fungus disease spreads by spores in soil mixture	roots swollen and rotting; leaves grey-green and wilt	dip roots of transplant in mixture of 60g pure calomel per 0·61 (2oz per pint) water before planting. Destroy infected plants; do not plant in infected soil for at least 7 years
Flea beetle *turnip, swede and other cabbage family plants*	tiny blue-black or black and yellow beetles which hop	eat small round holes in leaves of seedlings and young plants	dust leaves with derris
Greenfly *universal*	tiny green insects in clusters on tips of new shoots and underside of leaves; may also be pink, grey, bluish or cream	new shoots stunted, leaves curled and discoloured	remove with finger and thumb; spray bioresmethrin

Prevention and cure

Trouble	Appearance	Damage	Cure
Grey mould *(Botrytis cinerea)* *universal*	grey furry mould on leaves and stems	leaves turn yellow and rot, stems brown and wither	remove affected parts; spray benomyl
Leafminer *celery, celeriac, parsley*	minute maggot inside leaf tissue; mainly young plants	pale brown blisters and tunnels on leaves, which wither	remove affected leaves; spray remainder with malathion if bad attack
Mildew	white powdery patches on upper side of leaf, and on stems and fruit	leaves wilt and die, new shoots stunted fruit rots	remove infected parts; spray benomyl, but on lettuce use zineb
Onion white rot *leeks, shallot, garlic also*	white fluffy growth on base of onion bulb	yellow leaves, plant wilts, roots rot, then bulb	destroy infected plants; do not plant in infected soil for 10 years; dust soil before sowing with 4% calomel dust
Onion fly *leeks, shallot also*	tiny white maggots; adult fly like housefly	maggots feed in bulb of young plants and seedlings, which wilt;	treat as carrot fly
Parsnip canker	reddish brown or black patches on shoulder of root	root rots in infected areas	improve soil drainage; use resistant variety; sow in mid spring
Pea moth	tiny white maggots; adult moths grey-brown, 6mm(¼in) long	maggots feed on peas in pod	spray fenitrothion 7–10 days after start of flowering if trouble previous year

Prevention and cure

Trouble	Appearance	Damage	Cure
Potato blight *tomatoes also*	brown-black patches on leaves and stems, brown tubers and fruits	leaves and stems die, tubers and fruits rot	apply protective spray of Bordeaux Mixture at 3-week intervals from early July
Potato scab	dark raised rough patches on skin of tuber	not serious; tuber does not rot	removed when peeling for cooking
Red spider mite *universal but more likely on greenhouse crops*	minute red or yellowish insects on undersides of leaves, together with webbing	leaves speckled yellow/grey/brown, wither; plants stunted, cease to grow	spray derris or malathion; destroy worst infected leaves
Slugs and snails	well-known; underground slugs black	eat holes in leaves, stems, fruits, roots and tubers	use 15cm(6in) wide bands of grit round plants; scatter methiocarb pellets on soil; improve drainage
Whitefly *cabbage, tomato*	tiny white mothlike adults; young are transparent scales on underside of leaf	leaves curled, sticky, greyish eventually die; plants stunted; black mould grows on leaf	destroy worst affected parts; spray bioresmethrin on remainder
Wireworm *roots and tubers, especially potato and carrot*	yellow and shiny, up to 2·5cm(1in) long, slow moving	tunnels in tubers and roots which then rot	trap with slices of carrot/potato on skewers in soil; treat soil with diazinon before sowing/planting

Buying seeds

All vegetables can be grown from seed, and the majority are best started in this way. Seeds are the cheapest form in which to buy them and are supplied from garden shops and centres, and the garden departments of large stores.

You can also buy them mail-order from specialist seedsmen, who publish seed catalogues listing and describing many varieties. Ordering from such a catalogue gives you more choice, as well as information about each variety.

If you do not have time or facilities for growing from seed, many vegetables can be bought as young plants from local garden centres and some large stores. These include the cabbage family (except swedes and turnips), tomatoes, leeks, peas and beans, celery, cucumbers and marrows, and sometimes in some areas, aubergine, peppers and sweetcorn.

Vegetables are also grown from tubers or bulbs, i.e. potatoes, Jerusalem artichokes, onion and shallot sets, and garlic. Globe artichokes and asparagus are sold as small plants. Asparagus can be grown from seed, but needs three years before it can be cropped. Many of this type of plant can also be ordered from seedsmen, though plants will, of course, cost more than seeds.

When buying plants, look for specimens with leaves of good, even, deep green, and with plenty of root. Healthy young roots are mostly white. Cabbage family plants should have about four leaves; tomato plants should be about 12cm(5in) tall. None of them should be leggy and drawn. Celery plants, when young, are usually rather a pale green.

Orders for seeds or plants are best placed early in winter for delivery as required.

PACKAGED SEED

Buying seeds
Most packaged seed is very reliable, but it is worth checking a few points when buying seed:
1. The packet should be made of metal foil, or contain an inner seed packet of foil.
2. The date of packing should be stated.
3. The packet should be perfectly sealed and contain no dirt.

CARROT

MARROW

25·11·80

Storing seeds

If you want to save your own seed for the next generation of plants, you should protect the seed-pods on the plants from rain so that they ripen quickly, and then collect them on a warm dry day. Usually, the pods will have become light brown in colour and will be dry and crackly to the touch when ripe, and it should be possible to hear the seeds rattling about inside. Once collected, they should be shaken clear of the pods on to paper or muslin. Separate them from any remaining bits of leaf, stalk, bristle and so on – this can be done with a household sieve – and put them into air-tight containers which are completely light proof.

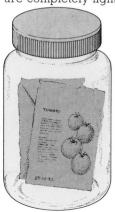

Storing the seed
The addition of silica gel to the containers, or a few grains of rice, will absorb any moisture. Vaseline smeared round the join between lid and container will improve the seal. Put the containers in a cool, dry place and remember to label and date them.

THE LIFE OF A SEED

Germination ▶
The factors which govern germination are moisture and warmth. When the seed has absorbed sufficient water, in soil which is consistently at the right temperature, it will swell and split releasing the plumule, which grows upwards, and the radicle which is the beginning of the root system.

The seedling ▶
The first leaves are the plumule leaves. When these are established and the radicle has produced rootlets, the plant begins to draw its food from the soil.

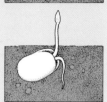

The maturing plant ▶
When the plant has produced some true leaves it is no longer a seedling. At this stage, many vegetables can be transplanted. It now draws its food in the form of mineral salts from the soil, and carbondioxide from the atmosphere.

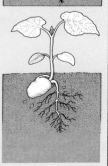

Frames and cloches

The protection from cold that glass or plastic frames and cloches supply is considerable, and they can be of great use to the vegetable gardener.

Frames can be used to protect boxes or pots of seeds and seedlings, or the seeds can be sown directly into the soil or compost of the frame. Plants started early in this way will then provide crops earlier than usual.

They can be used for forcing vegetables early in winter by making a hotbed in them from rotting manure; they can be used for starting peppers, tomatoes and aubergines early, removing the frame light when the plants get too tall. Some plants can be planted direct in the frame and left there throughout their lives.

Frames can also be used to protect through the winter pea seedlings sown in pots, and lettuce grown direct in the frame.

For best results, the frames should be in a sunny place, protected from north and east, preferably by a wall.

Cloches can be used in similar ways but they do not keep the plants as warm. Their advantage is mobility. They can be transferred from one crop to another as the vegetables are harvested.

Points to look for

1. Sound, durable construction – either wood or aluminium.
2. An effective ventilating prop.
3. Thermostatic control of the heating.
4. Air, or soil, warming cables (an under-soil heating plate can be just as effective).
5. Glass lights will give the greatest benefit, but plastic ones are safer.

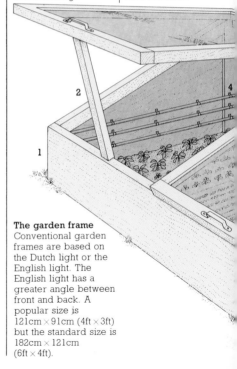

The garden frame
Conventional garden frames are based on the Dutch light or the English light. The English light has a greater angle between front and back. A popular size is 121cm × 91cm (4ft × 3ft) but the standard size is 182cm × 121cm (6ft × 4ft).

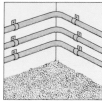

Air warming
Low voltage cables fixed to the sides of the frame.

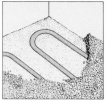

Soil warming
Under soil cables can operate, like the side-fixed type, through mains power or transformer.

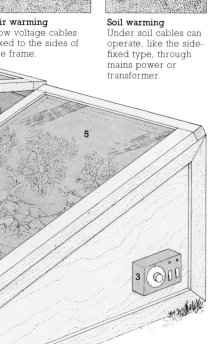

PORTABLE CLOCHES

Frames and cloches are available in a wide variety of sizes, types and prices, and they can of course be home-made. The examples shown here are, perhaps, the most widely used and easily available.

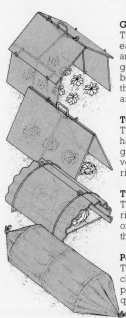

Glass barn
This type of cloche is easily moved to another part of the garden, but glass can be risky – especially if there are children around.

Tent cloche
Traditionally, these have been made of glass but modern versions are made in rigid plastic.

Tunnel cloche
This type, made from rigid plastic, has some of the advantages of the tent cloche.

Polythene tunnel
This flexible type is cheap, but the polythene deteriorates quickly.

General care

Vegetables can be grown by any one with a little bit of gardening experience and the help of seed-packet instructions. But to grow first class crops year after year, it is essential that the soil is in really good condition, fertile and crumbly.

Very few soils are like this naturally, but you can get yours into this condition with regular additions of rotted organic matter, such as garden compost, farm manure, spent mushroom compost, seaweed, leafmould and so on. An average dressing for an average soil is about 4½kg per sq.m (10lb per sq.yd).

Sandy, stony or chalky soils will need up to 8½kg per sq.m (19lb per sq.yd); heavy, clay-based soils about 3½kg (8lb).

When the crops are growing, cover the soil round them with a layer of the same materials about 1·2–2·5cm(½–1in) thick. This is called a mulch. Put it on when the soil is moist; it will conserve the moisture and prevent weed growth.

You will also need to add powder or granulated proprietary fertilizers to improve the food content, but after some years it should be possible to decrease these applications considerably.

Soil testing
Take a small amount of soil and press it between your fingers. A good soil will be light brown, crumbly and workable, but will hold together without being sticky.

Mulching
Mulching is a method of keeping moisture in the soil, inhibiting weed growth and retaining warmth. Peat, leaves and compost are the best mulches.

Once the crops are established, they should never run out of moisture. If dry weather occurs, water after a few days of it. Use a sprinkler and leave it on each patch of ground for 2 hours. Do this at 4-day intervals or so, depending on your soil type and the degree of heat, until rain comes. Lack of water, or heavy watering after drought, produces tough vegetables, split fruit, cracked roots and tubers. Drought results in bolting (running to flower) and small crops.

Do the first thinning of the seedlings as soon as they can be handled.

Transplant only the healthy, well-shaped young plants, and get rid of weeds by hoeing when they are young or spraying with paraquat, before they overwhelm the crops. Choose the right varieties for the right season. Use tall crops to shade those that might run to flower, if in sun.

Remember that the largest are by no means the tastiest vegetables. The smaller ones will be more tender, juicier and better flavoured.

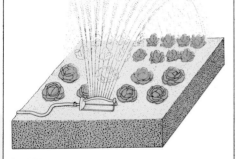

Sprinklers
Sprinkling is the best way of getting a reasonable quantity of water into the ground during dry spells. Sprinkler units can be bought as hose attachments.

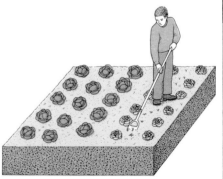

Hoeing
The only really effective way of restricting weed growth when plants are young is to hoe regularly between the rows. A Dutch hoe is best for this.

41

Globe artichoke

Site	sunny, sheltered from wind
Soil	fertile, moist, well-drained, slightly acid or alkaline
Soil preparation	double-dig late autumn early winter, mix in rotted organic matter; rake in good general compound fertilizer at manufacturer's recommended rates about a week before planting
Plant	mid spring at 1·2m(4ft) square; water in; provide 1·5m(5ft) stakes if not sheltered
Feed	give general liquid fertilizer at regular intervals from late spring to early autumn
Water	heavily in dry weather
Mulch	established plants in late spring
Weed	young plants; mature plants will spread sufficiently to cover the space between plants
Harvest	mid summer–mid autumn; cut main heads first, then heads on sideshoots; cut just as tips of scales begin to open; in first summer take only 2–3 heads, remove others when just formed
Store	surplus heads will keep a few days if cut off with 30cm(1ft) of stem pushed into damp sand

Recommended varieties

Vert de Laon

Green Globe

Grande Beurré

Earwig

Troubles
Occasionally greenfly, blackfly earwigs in heads (place in salt water before cooking). Petal blight – brown spots on scales of head – in cold wet summers. Spray with zineb as flower buds form.

Note
Increase from rooted suckers at base of plant, cut off when 25cm (10in) tall and plant in mid autumn. Discard plants after five years. Protect all plants from severe cold.

Jerusalem artichoke

Site	sun or shade
Soil	any soil unless waterlogged or dry
Soil preparation	in late autumn–early winter single-dig, mix in rotted organic matter; rake in a compound potassium-high fertilizer at manufacturer's rates or wood-ash at 180g per sq.m (6oz per sq.yd) a week before planting
Plant	late winter–early spring; set egg-shaped tubers, or large ones cut up so that they have three 'eyes' or buds, in holes 15cm(6in) deep and 60cm(2ft) apart; shoots appear in 2–4 weeks; provide 1·8m(6ft) stout stakes in windy areas
Water	heavily in dry weather
Weed	while plants are young
Harvest	from late autumn to late winter; leave in the ground until required
Store	dig some up in early winter before the ground becomes hard frozen and store in peat or dry sand in the dark
Note	cut stems down to 30cm(1ft) in late autumn, leaving stump to mark site for digging; dig out all tubers at the end of winter otherwise the remaining ones sprout and become a nuisance

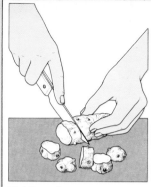

Dividing tubers
When preparing tubers for planting, cut them into pieces with a kitchen knife so that each segment has three "eyes".

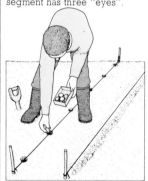

Planting
Segments should be set 15cm (6in) deep and 60cm (2ft) apart. Jerusalem artichokes are amenable to any type of soil.

Asparagus

Site	sunny, not too exposed to wind
Soil	deep, moist, fertile and well-drained, containing some sand, neutral to slightly alkaline
Soil preparation	double-dig in late winter or early spring and mix in rotted organic matter; remove completely all perennial weeds; prepare an area 1·2m(4ft) wide for 2 rows of plants; fork over the soil a few days before planting and, if soil is acid, add lime to make the soil neutral in its reaction
Plant	early or mid spring; dig a trench 30cm(1ft) deep and one spade wide; for one row, make a rounded ridge of soil 23cm(9in) deep down the centre, using the dug-out topsoil, put the plants on the ridge and spread the roots down the sides; space them 45cm(1½ft) apart each way; cover the plants with 7cm(3in) soil, and fill in trench completely
Stake	supply 90cm(3ft) supports in windy areas when cutting shoots has finished
Weed	keep clear of weeds at all times, especially when plants are young
Feed	feed with rock salt (agricultural salt) at 60g per sq.m (2oz per sq.yd) in mid spring, late spring and early summer; apply wood-ash at 120g per sq.m (4oz per sq.yd) in late winter, and soot (if available) in early spring at the same rate

Planting
A well prepared trench is essential to asparagus: they need good drainage around the crowns. Some experienced growers recommend growing the plants in slightly raised beds

Weeding
Because asparagus occupies the same plot for year after year it is important to ensure that the ground is as near weed free as possible.

44

Asparagus

Mulch	in mid autumn with rotted organic matter
Water	heavily in dry weather
Harvest	late spring – early summer; cut the shoots (spears) when 7–10cm (3–4in) tall; cut well below the soil surface; cut all shoots that appear; use the thin ones for soup, or discard; do not take any shoots in the first or second seasons of planting; in the third take only a few of the first shoots to appear
Troubles	asparagus beetle: grubs feed inside shoots and on leaves, plants seriously weakened; spray derris several times when first noticed; destroy infested stems; violet root rot: foliage yellows prematurely, roots die; plants should be dug up and destroyed; use new site
Varieties	Connover's Colossal, Martha Washington
Note	Cut down stems in mid autumn to stubs; plant at least 24 plants for a family of four Asparagus will give a worthwhile crop in a comparatively small plot and, because of the market price of fresh asparagus, gives excellent value for money as a home-grown vegetable. It is, however, a long term crop and one which requires a well-prepared and maintained bed. Feeding in spring and summer is especially important because asparagus will occupy the same ground for many years.

Cutting back
After the shoots have been taken in June, the foliage will grow vigorously – do not cut it back until October.

Harvesting
Asparagus is a luxury crop, and a long term one, but yields can be very good if soil and plants are kept in good condition.

Aubergine

Site	greenhouse, or sheltered warm site backed by south-facing wall
Soil	well-drained fertile soil
Soil preparation	single-dig a month before planting and mix in rotted organic matter; rake in a compound potash-high fertilizer at manufacturer's rates, or wood-ash at 180g per sq.m (6oz per sq.yd) a week before planting
Sow	early spring in seed compost at a temperature of 18°C(65°F) germination time 14–21 days; sow thinly in seed-trays, or two in 5cm(2in) peat pot or block and remove the weaker when potting on
Pot	when 3 or 4 leaves formed, into 7cm(3in) pot; use standard potting compost
Plant	late spring–early summer outdoors after hardening off, protect from late frosts; mid–late spring in greenhouse; space the plants at 60cm(2ft) apart; water in after planting; supply 90cm(3ft) stake
Water	heavily in dry weather in open ground
Harvest	late summer–early autumn, when fruit has stopped swelling; the purple varieties will be coloured from the time of setting; cut stems, do not pull off
Varieties	Burpee Hybrid, Early Long Purple

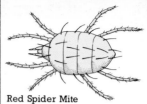

Red Spider Mite
Greatly magnified

Troubles
Red spider mite in hot climates; grey mould in cool ones; sometimes greenfly and whitefly, slugs on young plants.

Potting
When 3 or 4 leaves are formed, put into 7cm (3 in) pot using a standard potting compost.

Training young plants
Break off the growing tip when 15cm (6in) tall, just above a pair of leaves; allow only 4 or 5 fruits per plant.

Note
Aubergines are best grown in greenhouses in temperate climates, where they can be treated as tomatoes.

Broad bean

Site	sun or a little shade
Soil	deep, moist heavy soil, slightly alkaline
Soil preparation	single-dig late autumn–early winter and mix in rotted organic matter; lime if required six weeks later; rake in superphosphate of lime at 60g per sq.m (2oz per sq.yd) a week before sowing
Sow	early and mid spring; space seeds 23cm(9in) apart in 2 staggered rows 15cm(9in) apart in a wide shallow trench 5cm(2in) deep; cover with 2·5cm(1in) soil; germination time 8–14 days; sow extra seeds for transplanting because germination is erratic
Support	as they grow, with posts and two wires 30 and 60cm(1 and 2ft) above the ground along the rows on each side; dwarf varieties will not need support
Weed	frequently in early stages
Water	heavily in dry weather, especially late sown crops
Harvest	late spring–mid summer; from base of stem upwards; pick when sizable beans can be felt in pods
Troubles	blackfly on tips of main shoots
Varieties	Express, Imperial Green Windsor (both 60–90cm/2–3ft tall. The Sutton 30cm/1ft)

Support
Using posts and wires is easier and more secure than providing a stake for each plant.

Blackfly
These pests often do not appear until the plants have reached a fair size. The simplest way to dispose of them is to remove the tips on which they feed.

Note
Broad beans can be sown in late autumn for spring cropping, but only where winters will be mild. Use the variety Aquadulce and prepare soil in mid autumn.

French bean

Site	sunny, sheltered from cold, this crop is tender
Soil	any good soil, neutral to slightly alkaline
Soil preparation	add lime in winter if needed; single-dig the soil in early spring and clear off weeds; mix in rotted organic matter; about a week before planting rake in sulphate of potash at 14g per sq.m (½oz per sq.yd)
Sow	early spring in warm districts, mid–late spring in others; protect at night until germinated, also during the day in cold weather; space seed 23cm(9in) apart, in double rows 30cm(1ft) apart; sow 5cm(2in) deep; germination time 10–21 days
Support	supply short pea sticks about 30cm(1ft) long or use wire strung along row on short stakes; beans trailing on the soil will be eaten by slugs
Feed	supply liquid fertilizer occasionally
Water	heavily in dry weather
Harvest	early summer–early autumn; about 10–12 weeks after sowing, when pods are about 10cm(4in) long; pick every 2 or 3 days
Troubles	slugs, capsids
Varieties	Tendergreen, Glamis (for cold districts), Flair, The Prince

Pea sticks
French or dwarf beans can be grown unsupported, but in practice they tend to lean as the pods form. Pea sticks will prevent this.

Thinning
To ensure fully germinated rows, sow every 10–12cm (4–5in) and thin out alternate plants.

Haricot beans
Haricot beans can be obtained by leaving the pods on the plant until they dry and split. Take the beans from the pods and spread them on trays to dry in a warm, airy place. Store in airtight containers.

Runner bean

Site	sunny, sheltered from wind
Soil	deep, moist, fertile, slightly acid to slightly alkaline
Soil preparation	in late autumn or early winter, single-dig a 60cm(2ft) wide trench if the soil is medium to heavy, double-dig if it is sandy; mix in rotted organic matter; apply lime if necessary a few weeks later; if the soil is sandy, fork in more organic matter to topsoil in early spring; for all soils, rake in 45g per sq.m (½oz per sq.yd) 2 weeks before sowing
Sowing	sow seeds outdoors in late spring in V-shaped drills 5cm(2in) deep; space the seed 23cm(9in) apart in two rows 30cm(1ft) apart; protect with cloches until young plants growing well; in warm districts, sow seed in mid spring
Weed	while plants are young
Feed	liquid fertilizer, weekly, on medium to light soils
Water	heavily in dry weather, otherwise flowers will not set
Mulch	if grown in sandy or stony soil, in early summer
Harvest	mid summer–mid autumn; 12–14 weeks after sowing, when pods are 12–17cm(5–7in) long; pick every few days

Recommended varieties

Achievement

Best of All

Sunset

Scarlet Emperor

Supporting plants
Supply 1 2m (7ft) stake to each plant. Cross near the top and tie to horizontal stakes. Secure with guy ropes and short stakes. If the supports are not very secure, summer gales may blow down the entire crop.

Troubles
Slugs eat shoots; bean beetles eat seeds in ground – sow only clean seeds; sparrows peck off flowers.

Note
Leave the roots in the ground at the end of the season – they are rich in nitrogen.

Beetroot

Site	sunny
Soil	best on sandy, well-drained soil; neutral to very slightly alkaline
Soil preparation	in early spring, single-dig medium to light soils; if round or globe varieties are to be grown single dig in late autumn–early winter; double-dig heavy soils and for long varieties; do not add organic matter; remove all large stones; lime in mid winter if necessary; rake in general compound fertilizer a week before sowing at 60g per sq.m(2oz per sq.yd)
Sow	sow salad beet in mid spring–mid summer at 4-week intervals; space seed 5cm(2in) apart and 2·5cm(1in) deep with 30cm(1ft) between rows; sow beets for storage and maincrop in early summer; germination time 12–24 days
Thin	remove all but the strongest seedling from each cluster when large enough to handle; thin again to 10cm(4in) spacing when 5cm(2in) tall for salad beet, and to 15cm(6in) when 15cm(6in) tall for main-crop and store varieties
Weed	frequently in early stages
Water	keep well supplied with water
Harvest	salad beet about 11 weeks after sowing, when 2·5–7cm(1–3in) diameter; maincrop and store beet in early and mid autumn when 7–15cm(3–6in) long

Recommended varieties

Salad varieties
Detroit Little Ball
Boltardy
Avonearly
Maincrop and storage
Globe
Cook's Delight
Detroit Little Ball

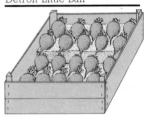

Storage
Store in dry sand or peat, in the dark, protected from frost. Lift the crop with a fork and shake the soil from the roots. Twist off the tops to avoid damaging the roots which will "bleed" if injured.

Broccoli

Site	sunny, free from wind
Soil	deep, moist, slightly heavy, slightly alkaline
Soil preparation	double-dig in late autumn–early winter; mix in rotted organic matter if previous crop was not manured; lime a few weeks later if necessary; rake in a potash-high fertilizer a week before planting
Sow	early and mid spring; sow thinly 1·2cm(½in) deep in drills 15cm(6in) apart, protect with cloche in cold weather; germination time 7–12 days
Thin	when large enough to handle, to 7cm(3in) apart in 2 stages
Transplant	early–mid summer when 4–5 leaves present; space 60–75cm(2–2½ft) apart and plant firmly with lowest leaf just above soil; water hole before planting
Stake	use 90cm(3ft) stakes
Weed	frequently when young
Water	keep well supplied with water when plants are young and in dry weather
Mulch	shortly after transplanting
Harvest	late winter–early spring; when floret shoots about 15cm(6in) long; start with top florets
Varieties	Early and Late Purple, Early and Late White (both sprouting types)

Common troubles

Cabbage White caterpillars

Birds – *at all times*

Cabbage root fly

Flea beetle

Mealy aphis *grey-white greenfly*

Club root *see below*

Club root
A soil-borne fungus which causes roots to swell and rot. The leaves turn grey-brown and wilt. Burn infected plants, lime the soil and plant no brassicas for three years.

Calabrese
This is an Italian variety of sprouting broccoli with large, tender green sprouts. Sow in late spring where it is to crop. Thin to 38 cm (15in); harvest about 14 weeks after sowing.

Brussels sprouts

Site	sunny, sheltered from wind
Soil	deep, moist, slightly heavy, slightly alkaline
Soil preparation	double-dig in late autumn–early winter; mix in rotted organic matter if previous crop was not manured; lime a few weeks later if necessary; rake in general compound fertilizer, slightly higher in potash and phosphate than nitrogen, about 10 days before planting
Sow	outdoors in early–mid spring; sow thinly 1·2cm($\frac{1}{2}$in) deep in drills 15cm(6in) apart; protect with cloche in severe weather; germination time 7–12 days
Thin	when large enough to handle, to 10cm(4in) apart, in 2 stages
Transplant	early–mid summer, when 4–5 leaves are present; space 45cm(1$\frac{1}{2}$ft) apart in the row, and 60–75cm(2–2$\frac{1}{2}$ft) apart between rows; water hole before planting and plant firmly, with lowest leaf just above the soil
Stake	supply 90cm(3ft) stake for each plant at planting time
Weed	frequently when young
Water	heavily in drought, especially when plants are young
Mulch	shortly after transplanting

Harvest
From early autumn to late winter, Cut lowest sprouts first, when about 2.5cm(1in) in diameter.

Note
Sprouts will be loose and 'blown' if the plants are grown in newly dug, loose soil. Too much nitrogen and too little water when young will have the same effect.

Troubles *see Cabbage page 54*

Cabbage

Site	sun or partial shade
Soil	any moist but not waterlogged soil; slightly alkaline
Soil preparation	single-dig in late autumn–early winter; mix in lime a few weeks later if soil is acid; rake in potash-high compound fertilizer at manufacturer's rates about 10 days before planting; for spring cabbage, rake in 120g per sq.m(4oz per sq.yd) of hoof and hornmeal
Sow	seed for autumn and winter cabbage outdoors in mid and late spring 1·2cm(½in) deep, 4cm(1½in) apart, in rows 15cm(6in) apart in a seed bed; sow spring cabbage in mid–late summer in the same way; germination time 7–12 days
Thin	when plants are large enough to handle, to 7cm(3in) spacing
Transplant	when 4 or 5 leaves present; space autumn and winter cabbage 45–60cm(1½–2ft) apart, spring cabbage 30cm(1ft); water soil before planting and plant firmly
Weed	frequently when plants are young
Feed	give nitro-chalk at 42g per sq.m(1½oz per sq.yd) to spring cabbage in late winter and early spring
Water	keep well supplied with water in dry weather, especially when plants are young

Recommended varieties

Autumn and winter varieties
Babyhead
Christmas Drumhead
Holland Late winter White
Red Cabbage
Blood Red
Rugby Ball
Spring cabbage
Durham Early
Spring Bounty

See also page 54

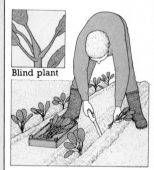

Blind plant

Transplanting
When transplanting cabbage plants, or any of the brassica group, watch for signs of club root (grey-green wilted leaves and poor root structure). Look also for blind plants – plants that are swollen and distorted at the growing point. Do not transplant cabbages which have more or less than 4 or 5 leaves.

Cabbage

Harvest	autumn cabbage between early and late autumn; winter varieties including Savoys from late autumn to late winter; spring cabbage from late winter to late spring; red cabbage early autumn to early winter; cut when the heads have stopped expanding and are firm; do not let spring cabbage form hearts
Store	winter cabbage by digging up and hanging upside down with roots attached in dark, frost-free shed; Dutch white cabbage on a wire rack in similar conditions
Troubles	birds at all stages; cabbage white butterfly caterpillar, cabbage root-fly, mealy aphis (greyish-white greenfly), whitefly, club-root, flea-beatle
Varieties	*autumn and winter cabbage:* Babyhead, Christmas Drumhead, Pride of the Market, Holland Late Winter White (for coleslaw); *Savoy cabbage* (also winter): January King, Ormskirk, Wirosa; *red cabbage:* Blood Red, Rugby Ball; *spring cabbage:* Durham Early, April, Offenham Spring Bounty
Notes	hearted spring cabbage can be obtained by planting at 45cm(1½ft) spacing, and leaving to grow a little longer; cabbages can be cropped in summer by sowing thinly in late winter or early spring in cold frames, transplanting in mid to late spring, spaced 30–38cm(12–15in) apart each way, and keeping protected in cold and frosty weather; summer varieties are: Golden Acre, Hispi, Earliest

Note
Cabbages will only produce solid compact heads if planted on firm soil, planted firmly, kept watered in dry weather when young, and given sparing quantities of nitrogen.

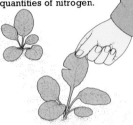

Plant firmly
After planting test the firmness by pulling one of the leaves. There should be no movement at all in the stem or roots.

Storage
If winter cabbages are to be stored by hanging upside down in a dry shed, make sure that they are in sound condition and not affected by rot.

Carrot

Site	open or sunny
Soil	well-drained, containing sand, free from stones
Soil preparation	single-dig late autumn–early winter; rake in potash-high fertilizer 1–2 weeks before sowing; use ground manured for previous crop
Sow	outdoors, early spring–mid summer; sow very thinly 6mm(¼in) deep in rows 15cm(6in) apart for short types, 30–38cm(12–15in) apart for intermediate types; germination time 17–24 days
Thin	short types and for salads, in stages to 5cm(2in) apart; intermediate types, main-crops and for store, to 15cm(6in); start to thin when seedlings are large enough to handle
Weed	frequently when young
Water	well in dry weather, otherwise roots split and become tough
Harvest	late spring–mid autumn; short and salad types 10–12 weeks after sowing, remainder 14–18 weeks
Store	lift in autumn when leaves start to yellow; clean the roots, cut off the leaves, and store in layers in dry sand or peat in a box in a dark, frost-proof place

Recommended varieties

Stump rooted types

Amsterdam Forcing

Chantenay Red-cored

Parisian Rondo *completely round*

Early Nantes

The above are suitable for early crops, forcing and salads.

Chantenay Red-cored Favourite

Royal Chantenay

Scarla

The above are suitable for maincrop and storage

Intermediate types

Autumn King

Early Giant

New Red Intermediate

St. Valery

Juwarot

All are suitable for maincrops and storage.

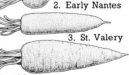

1. Parisian Rondo

2. Early Nantes

3. St. Valery

Troubles
Carrot-fly, greenfly, wireworms; avoid bruising the foliage – the smell attracts carrot-fly.

Cauliflower, summer

Site	sunny, sheltered from wind, no frost pockets
Soil	moist, well-drained, rich neutral to slightly alkaline
Soil preparation	single-dig mid autumn–early winter, mix in rotted organic matter; add lime a few weeks later if required; early in late winter, mix in a little more organic matter if the soil is sandy; about a week before planting rake in a general compound fertilizer at 120g per sq.m(4oz per sq.yd)
Sow	early–late spring and protect with cloches against frosty or chilly weather; sow seed 4cm(1½in) apart, 1·2cm(½in) deep in rows 23cm(9in) apart; germination time 7–12 days
Thin	alternate plants when leaves are touching
Transplant	when 4–5 leaves present; water hole before planting, plant firmly up to lowest leaf; space 45cm(1½ft) apart, with rows 60cm(2ft) apart for summer maturing kinds, and 60cm(2ft) apart each way for autumn and early winter kinds
Weed	frequently when young
Feed	summer crops with sulphate of ammonia at 15–30g per sq.m(½–1oz per sq. yd) about 5 weeks after planting, and water in
Troubles	Birds, cabbage white butterfly, caterpillars, flea beetle, club root, cabbage root-fly, mealy aphis

Recommended varieties

Summer varieties

All Year Round

Snow King

Snowcap

Autumn varieties

Kangaroo

Brisbane

Autumn Giant

Curd should be creamy white and closely packed

Harvest
18–24 weeks after sowing, when the inner leaves no longer cover the curd.

Mulching
Plants can be mulched generously instead of feeding, but must then be well watered.

Notes
Early summer cauliflowers can be obtained by sowing in heat in late winter and planting out in mid spring with protection.

Cauliflower, winter

(heading broccoli)

Site	sunny or open, free from frost pockets, sheltered from wind
Soil	moist, fertile, well-drained, slightly alkaline
Soil preparation	single-dig in late autumn–early winter; do not manure, but grow on soil manured for previous crop; lime if required a few weeks later; rake in superphosphate at 42g per sq.m (1½oz per sq.yd) and sulphate of potash at 21g per sq.m (¾oz per sq.yd) before sowing in the seed-bed, do *not* apply to the planting site
Sow	outdoors in late spring or early summer, 1·2cm(½in) deep, in rows 15cm(6in) apart; sow thinly; germination time 7–12 days
Thin	when large enough to handle, to a final spacing of 10cm(4in)
Transplant	when 4–5 leaves present; water hole before planting, plant firmly up to lowest leaf; space 60–75cm(2–2½ft) apart each way
Weed	keep clear of weeds at all times
Water	frequently in dry weather, especially when young
Harvest	early winter–late spring; 32–40 weeks after sowing, when curd is fully exposed and leaves no longer cover it; the curd should be white and will discolour if too matured or frosted

Recommended varieties

mid-late winter maturing
Angers No 1
Angers No 2
Westmarsh Early
Spring maturing
Walcheren Winter Birchington
Walcheren Winter Manston

Ridging
In early autumn draw the soil up along the plants from north to south. Bank the soil up to the lowest leaf to ensure good drainage and support.

Protection
Protect curds in severe weather by half breaking one or two outer leaves over them. Winter cauliflowers will survive most weather conditions and crop in late winter and spring.

Troubles
See page 56

57

Celeriac

Site	sunny, some shelter
Soil	moist, slightly heavy
Soil preparation	single-dig in late winter–early spring, and mix in rotted organic matter
Sow	seed indoors in warmth in early spring; use a good seed compost, and sow seed in boxes or 3 in a 5cm(2in) peat pot or block; germination time 12–21 days
Prick out	when three leaves present, into individual small pots, or 5cm(2in) apart in a seed box; reduce 3 seedlings to the strongest one
Transplant	late spring after hardening off, but protect in cold weather; plant 30cm(1ft) apart in rows 30–38cm(12–15in) apart; do not plant deeply
Water	keep well supplied with water in early and mid summer, even in cool conditions
Feed	liquid-feed regularly from mid summer–early autumn for extra large roots
Harvest	mid autumn–late winter; from the time when leaves begin to yellow; can be left in ground through winter, but may be eaten in soil by mice or rats
Store	cut off leaves, clean root of soil and store in layers in peat or sand in a dark, frost-free place
Varieties	Globus

Sowing
Seeds may be sown in an unheated greenhouse or frame in March or April.

Planting out
Plant in drills 5cm (2in) deep and 38cm (15in) apart. Apart from feeding, celeriac needs little attention until harvest time.

Frost protection
Cover the shoulder of the root with soil, if exposed, to prevent frost damaging the root.

Troubles
Occasionally celery fly (leaf miner)

Celery

Site	sunny
Soil	deep, moist, well-drained, fertile
Soil preparation	winter celery: double-dig a trench 38cm(15in) wide in late winter, and mix rotted organic matter into bottom of trench with soil to be returned to it; fill in trench to within 15cm(6in) of top; summer celery; single-dig and mix in rotted organic matter; rake in superphosphate at 60g per sq.m (2oz per sq.yd) for both kinds 2 weeks before planting
Sow	indoors during early spring in warmth; sow in seed boxes or 3 in a peat pot or block; use good seed compost, or potting compost; germination time 16–24 days
Transplant	late spring–early summer after hardening off but protect in cold weather; plant winter celery 23cm(9in) apart in double rows and summer celery in blocks, with 23cm(9in) between plants; for winter celery, clear the trench bottom of soil from the sides and water copiously before planting
Water	keep well watered at all times
Feed	liquid-feed with a low-nitrogen compound fertilizer from mid summer until early autumn
Harvest	summer celery: from late summer to middle of early autumn; winter celery: from mid autumn until late winter; remove earthed-up soil and lever plant out with fork

Recommended varieties

Summer varieties
Golden Self Blanching
American Green
Winter varieties
Giant White
Giant Red
Giant Pink

Blanching
To keep the stems white, earth up winter celery at 3-week intervals starting in late summer. Tie stems together and remove sideshoots before earthing. The soil should eventually reach the leaves. Surround summer celery with black plastic sheet or sacking.

Prick out
When 3 leaves are present, put seedlings singly into small pots.

Troubles
Slugs – keep them out of earthed-up plants; celery-fly; celery heart rot (brown and slimy) occurs if plants are injured before earthing.

Chicory

Site	sunny or a little shade
Soil	deep, light to medium, slightly alkaline
Soil preparation	double-dig in late autumn–early winter and mix in rotted organic matter; add lime if required in mid to late winter; if manured and prepared for a previous crop, fork a month or so before sowing
Sow	ordinary chicory outdoors in late spring, but sow Sugar Loaf in early and mid summer; do not sow in dry soil; sow seed 1.2cm($\frac{1}{2}$in) deep in rows 30–38cm(12–15in) apart
Thin	when large enough to handle and again, later, to a final spacing of 25cm(10in)
Cut down	remove flowering stems, if they appear, before flowering
Harvest	Sugar Loaf in early and mid autumn; chicons early winter onwards
Lift	varieties for chicons in late autumn; remove remains of leaves, trim main root back to 20cm(8in) long
Store	horizontally in cool conditions [maximum 7°C(45°F)], place layers in moist sand or peat in a box, until needed
Varieties	Sugar Loaf, *like cos lettuce*; Witloof, Red Verona, *forcing varieties*
Troubles	slugs; birds may attack seedlings

1. Cut off leaves about two inches above the root and trim the root back to about 20cm (8in) long.

2. Place the roots in moist peat, sand, or compost in containers; space them 7cm (3in) apart.

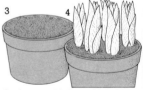

3. Cover with 5cm (2in) of filling material and keep in a completely dark place at 10–13°C (50–55°F).

4. Pull up roots 4–6 weeks later when chicons (leaves) are about 15cm (6in) tall.

Cress

Soil and site	sunny or some shade, very moist, fertile soil with good drainage
Soil preparation	in early spring fork an area about 1 metre (1 yard) square and mix in rotted organic matter; build up the sides of the bed 5cm(2in) above the surrounding soil; if the soil is heavy, dig it out 30cm(1ft) deep, and put a layer of drainage material in the base 10cm(4in) deep, then return soil mixed with grit
Cultivation	plant rooted cuttings 15–20cm(6–8in) apart in mid–late spring and keep shaded until established; use shoots from the greengrocer and root in water; flood the bed daily once established or use trickle irrigation through summer and early autumn; remove flowering heads; protect with cloches or frames in cold weather; harvest some weeks after planting; renew the bed every 4 or 5 years
American or Land Cress	plant or sow in late summer as well as spring; cultivation similar but protect only during severe cold
Mustard and Cress	grow indoors in temperature of 16–18°C(60–65°F); sow cress 3 days before mustard; half-fill a container with very moist peat, sow the seed thickly on this and press into the peat so that it is covered; put in the dark until germination occurs; if peat begins to dry before cutting, add more water; allow 8 days from sowing to cutting in summer, and 13 days in winter

Rooting
Watercress shoots bought from your greengrocer will root satisfactorily if stood in water for a few days.

Irrigation
Flood beds once a day, or use trickle irrigation (*see glossary*).

Mustard and cress
Sowing the cress 3 days before the mustard ensures that both will be ready for eating at the same time.

Cucumber
ridge or frame

Site	sheltered, warm, sunny or some shade
Soil	moist, fertile
Soil preparation	single-dig hole 60cm(2ft) square for each plant, half fill with rotted organic matter, and replace topsoil; spacing 45cm(1½ft) for climbing, or 75cm(2½ft) on the flat
Sow	indoors in warmth in mid spring; sow one seed on edge in a 5cm(2in) peat or other pot; cover with 1·2cm(½in) compost; use a good seed compost; germination time 3–9 days, depending on temperature
Pot	pot into 10cm(4in) pot 1 week after germination; use good potting compost
Plant	harden off and plant out in frame in late spring, or in the open under cloche
Train	break off growing tip of main shoot just above 6th leaf, that of sideshoots at 7th leaf; stop remainder to keep within space available; supply trellis if plants are to climb
Water	heavily in dry weather
Feed	with general compound fertilizer at 60g(2oz) per plant some weeks after planting
Harvest	late summer–mid autumn; 10–14 weeks after sowing, when about 15–17cm(6–9in) long
Varieties	Burpless Tasty Green, Perfection

GREENHOUSE CUCUMBERS

Recommended varieties
Butchers Disease-resisting
Femspot *all female flowers*
Telegraph Improved

Cultivation
Sow in heat, in late winter, and plant in the greenhouse border in early spring at a minimum temperature of 13°C (55°F). Train with a single stem on supports, and stop sideshoots at 2 leaves beyond fruit. Stop the main stem when it reaches the greenhouse roof. Keep the atmosphere very humid and give a thick layer of mulch to the plants once a month. Remove male flowers to prevent bitter tasting fruit. Harvest early summer – mid autumn.

Pinching out
Removing the growing tip when the plant has reached a good height, encourages the lateral shoots to grow.

Troubles
Red spider mite, whitefly, slugs, collar rot – stem rots near soil level due to water collecting at base of stem.

 **Endive**

Site	should have some shade
Soil	light, well-drained, fertile
Soil preparation	single-dig mid spring, use a site manured for a previous crop; if soil is very light, mix in rotted organic matter when digging; rake in general compound fertilizer at 60g per sq.m (2oz per sq.yd) a week before sowing
Sow	curly-leaved endive outdoors in early and mid summer, broad-leaved Batavian types outdoors in mid and late summer; sow thinly 1·2cm(½in) deep in rows 30–38cm(12–15in) apart; sow both types at 2-week intervals to provide a succession; germination time 3 days in warm weather
Thin	when 3 leaves present, and again to space the plants to 30cm(1ft)
Feed	liquid-feed every 10 days after 6 weeks from sowing until mature
Water	copiously in dry weather, otherwise it will run to flower
Protect	with cloches from early autumn
Harvest	early autumn–mid winter about 12 weeks after sowing
Troubles	slugs, especially when blanching plants
Varieties	Moss-curled, Batavian Green

Blanching

Cover curly-leaved types with cloches a few days before blanching to dry, then cover with a large saucer or dinner plate to blanch the centre leaves 2–3 weeks before required. Use a large inverted pot on the broad-leaved varieties, but remember to stop up the drainage hole. Cloches covered with black plastic sheet will do just as well. This method takes 3–4 weeks. In cold weather, replant Batavian endive in boxes of compost and keep in the dark.

1. Cover broad-leaved types with a plant pot.

2. Cover curly-leaved varieties with a dinner plate.

Garlic

Site	sunny, sheltered
Soil	sandy to medium soil, fertile
Soil preparation	single-dig about 4 weeks before planting, and mix in rotted organic matter; a week before planting rake in bonemeal at 60g per sq.m (2oz per sq.yd)
Plant	outdoors early in mid autumn or in early spring; space cloves 15cm(6in) apart and 5cm(2in) deep, in rows 30cm(1ft) apart; shoots appear 2–3 weeks later
Protect	with cloche in severe winter weather
Weed	keep clear of weeds, especially when young
Feed	autumn-planted cloves with potash-high compound fertilizer in mid spring, and with nitrogen-high fertilizer in mid summer; spring-planted cloves with potash-high fertilizer in early summer
Water	only when dry weather is prolonged
Train	remove flower stems before flowers open
Harvest	mid–late summer; when leaves begin to yellow; dig bulbs up, leave to dry in sun
Store	tie together in bunches and hang in dark, dry frostproof place
Notes	greengrocer's bulbs can be used; plant large cloves taken from the outside

Soil preparation
Garlic likes quite rich soil; the addition of bonemeal to previously prepared ground helps the formation of good sized bulbs.

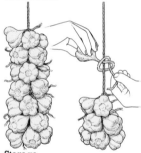

Storage
Leave the long stems on the garlic bulbs as they dry, and then tie them onto strings by knotting the dried stems. Start by putting a group of about four bulbs at the base of the string, then add individual bulbs.

Kale

Site	sunny or slightly shaded, shelter from wind
Soil	any reasonably good soil, neutral to slightly alkaline
Soil preparation	single-dig late autumn–early winter; mix in rotted organic matter if ground was not manured for previous crop; lime if required a few weeks later; rake in a potash-high fertilizer 2 weeks before planting; *for seed-bed*, rake in superphosphate of lime at 30g per sq.m (1oz per sq.yd) a week before sowing
Sow	outdoors in seed-bed in late spring–early summer, but sow variety Hungry Gap in mid summer where it is to crop; sow thinly 1·2cm(½in) deep, in rows 15cm(6in) apart for transplanting, 60cm(2ft) for direct-sown crop; germination time 7–12 days
Thin	at 3-leaf stage of seedling to 7cm(3in) apart; thin Hungry Gap in stages to a final spacing of 45cm(1½ft) between plants
Water	keep well supplied with water in dry weather, especially when young
Support	put in 90cm(3ft) stakes if site is windy
Feed	in late winter, with nitro-chalk at 30g per sq.m (1oz per sq.yd)
Harvest	late winter–late spring; take leaves and sideshoots while young, from top downwards

Recommended varieties

Dwarf Green Curled

Hungry Gap

Pentland Gap – *pick florets from this variety*

Transplant
Transplant when 4 or 5 leaves are present. Water the hole and plant firmly up to the first leaf; space 45–60cm(1½–2ft) apart.

Support
Plants will need a 90cm(3ft) stake if the site is windy.

Troubles
Birds at all stages; flea beetles, cabbage root-fly, club root, Cabbage White caterpillars, mealy aphis, slugs.

 # Kohl rabi

Site	sunny
Soil	medium to sandy, fertile, slightly acid to slightly alkaline
Soil preparation	single-dig in late autumn–early winter, and mix in rotted organic matter if ground was not manured for previous crop; add lime if required a few weeks later; rake in a compound fertilizer low in nitrogen a week before planting
Sow	white kinds outdoors from mid spring to early summer, purple kinds early summer–late summer; sow in succession at 2-week intervals for steady supply; sow 1·2cm($\frac{1}{2}$in) deep, in rows 45cm(1$\frac{1}{2}$in) apart; germination time 7–12 days
Thin	3-leaf seedlings in stages until 10–15cm(4–6in) apart
Water	keep well supplied with water to ensure rapid growth
Harvest	early summer–late winter, 8–12 weeks after sowing, when between 4 and 7cm(1$\frac{1}{2}$ and 3in) diameter (later they become tough and woody) pull alternate plants to start with; leave later-sown crops in soil or store
Store	dig up in late autumn and store in layers in dry sand or peat in dark frostproof place, but flavour will be less good

Rapid growth
The faster the plants grow, the more tender they are – so keep them growing with regular supplies of water.

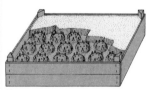

Storage
Kohl rabi can be stored in layers of sand or peat in boxes, but the flavour will gradually deteriorate.

Troubles
Flea beetle, birds at all stages; mice and rats may eat them in the ground.

Leek

Site	sun or shade
Soil	most soils; best results with moist, light fertile kinds
Soil preparation	single-dig in late autumn–early winter and mix in rotted organic matter; rake in a potash-high fertilizer a week before planting
Sow	outdoors in a seed-bed in early–late spring; sow thinly 6mm(¼in) deep in rows 15cm(6in) apart; germination time 14–21 days
Thin	very carefully when large enough to handle and then again to a 10cm(4in) spacing
Transplant	when about 20cm(8in) tall; make planting holes 15cm(6in) deep with a dibber, drop the leeks in and water to settle the soil over the roots; space the plants 15–23cm(6–9in) apart
Weed	frequently when young by hand or hoe; fill in holes gradually with soil at the same time
Water	keep well watered in dry weather
Feed	liquid-feed at 10-day intervals from mid summer until early autumn
Harvest	late autumn–late spring, when plants about 15–20cm(6–8in) tall
Troubles	occasionally onion fly

Recommended varieties

Musselburgh

Giant Winter

Prizetaker

Transplanting
Space plants 15–23cm (6–9in) apart, making holes with a dibber

Draw dry crumbly soil up against the stems.

Blanching
Draw the soil around the stems when the plants are 5cm (2in) high and repeat twice more in early autumn at 2-week intervals.

Note
Late sown leeks will provide a crop in spring; leeks sown in spring to crop where they grow will crop just as well but occupy the ground for as much as a year.

67

Lettuce

		Recommended Varieties

Site	sunny, shade at midday during summer
Soil	slightly heavy, moist but well-drained, slightly acid to slightly alkaline
Soil preparation	single-dig in late autumn–early winter for late spring and summer crops and mix in rotted organic matter, otherwise prepare soil a few weeks before sowing; add lime if required a few weeks later
Sow	1. outdoors from mid spring until end of mid summer at 2-week intervals to provide a succession in summer and early autumn 2. outdoors late summer and cloche from early autumn for mid–late autumn crops 3. under cloche or frame in early–mid autumn to overwinter and crop mid–late spring 4. under cloche or frame in late winter (in warm gardens) or early spring, removing protection when weather begins to warm, to crop late spring–early summer always use correct varieties for each cropping season; sow 1·2cm($\frac{1}{2}$in) deep in rows 30cm(1ft) apart for normal sized and large varieties; 23cm(9in) apart for small kinds; germination time 7–12 days
Thin	at 3-leaf stage and again to a final spacing of 30cm(1ft) and 23cm(9in) as above
Water	keep well supplied with water at all times otherwise they will run to flower in summer
Feed	liquid-feed at 7-day intervals with general compound fertilizer if soil is sandy

Recommended Varieties

Cabbage type summer/autumn

Avondefiance

Tom Thumb (*very small head*)

Cabbage type autumn/spring

Arctic King

Valdor

Loose leaf type summer/autumn

Salad Bowl

Grand Rapids

Cos summer

Romaine

Little Gem (*small and early*)

Cos autumn/spring

Lobjoit's Green

Winter Density (*intermediate*)

Cos

Cabbage

Loose Leaf

68

Lettuce

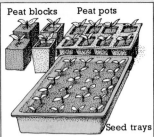

Peat blocks   Peat pots

Seed trays

Mulch	on sandy soil instead of feeding, after second thin
Harvest	early summer–early autumn, 8 weeks after sowing; late spring–early summer, mid to late autumn, 10–12 weeks after sowing; mid–late spring, 20 weeks for over-wintered kinds; cabbage kinds should have a round, solid heart – if they begin to form a point, they are about to run to flower
Troubles	slugs, grey mould (*Botrytis cinerea*), downy mildew (use zineb fungicide); greenfly or root aphids in dry weather
Varieties	*cabbage kinds* (summer and early autumn): All the Year Round, Avondefiance, Webb's Wonderful, Windermere, Tom Thumb; *cabbage kinds* (mid–late autumn and mid–late spring): Arctic King, Valdor, May Queen; *loose-leaf* (summer and early autumn): Salad Bowl, Grand Rapids; *cos* (summer): Romaine, Little Gem, Paris White; *cos* (mid–late autumn and mid–late spring): Lobjoit's Green Cos, Winter Density
Notes	lettuce can be sown in containers in warmth in late winter–early spring, then hardened off and planted out in early–mid spring for cropping in mid–late spring, but need a warm sheltered garden; loose-leaf kinds do not heart, leaves are harvested individually as required for several weeks

Spring lettuce
For an outdoor crop in mid- to late spring, sow in warmth in containers during late autumn/early winter and plant out in April or May after hardening off.

Irrigation
Lettuces need to grow quickly to be at their best; keep them well supplied with water especially in the summer months. Lettuces in frames or cloches during winter need very little water.

Onion

Site	sunny, sheltered
Soil	well-drained, light, fertile; slightly alkaline for spring onions
Soil preparations	single-dig late summer–early winter and use ground manured for previous crop; add lime if necessary a few weeks later; rake in half strength application of potash-high fertilizer 2 weeks before sowing or planting; soil must be firm but fine-textured
Sow	thinly outdoors early–mid spring but not in cold soil, put cloches over site 2 weeks in advance; sow seed 1·2cm($\frac{1}{2}$in) deep in rows 23cm(9in) apart; sow early autumn or late summer (Japanese varieties); germination time 21 days
Thin	when large enough to handle and again to a final spacing of 15cm(6in); do not thin spring or pickling onions
Plant	sets early–mid spring, (often more successful mid spring); plant so that half of set is in soil, 15cm(6in) apart, in rows 23cm(9in) apart; cut off withered brown leaves before planting
Weed	seedlings need very careful weeding
Harvest	spring-sown maincrop onions or sets late summer–early autumn; early-autumn sown varieties mid–late summer; Japanese varieties early–mid summer; tops will bend over and leaves begin to yellow when mature;

Sowing
Sow seeds thinly in 1cm ($\frac{1}{2}$in) drills; warm the soil, if necessary, with cloches for 2 weeks before sowing.

Thinning
Thin to a final spacing of 15cm (6in), but leave salad and pickling onions unthinned.

Planting sets
Make sure that only half of each bulb is in soil. Rows should be 23cm (9in) apart.

Onion

Harvest *continued*	dig up on a dry sunny day, clean off soil and hang on rack to dry for a few hours; spring onions late spring onwards when bulbs 1·2cm(½in) diameter; pickling kinds early summer when 1·2–2cm(½–¾in) diameter
Store	tie by tops in bundles and hang in dry, dark, frostproof place
Troubles	onion fly, white rot; birds when plants are young
Varieties	*for spring sowing:* Bedfordshire Champion, Ailsa Craig, Hygro; *for early autumn sowing:* Solidity, Ailsa Craig, Red Italian; *for sets:* Stuttgart Giant, Rijnsburger, Wijbo; *Japanese:* Extra Early Kaizuka, Senshyu; *pickling:* Paris Silverskin; *salad or spring onions:* White Lisbon, Giant Zittau
Notes	Japanese onions should be sown middle 2 weeks of late summer in average gardens, but in cold gardens during first 2 weeks, and in warm ones during last 2 weeks; this timing is crucial; Autumn-sown crops will store only until end of early winter; Japanese kinds last until end of early autumn, but do not store

Harvesting
When the leaves begin to turn yellow, bend the tops close to the bulb. This will advance ripening and increase weight. Leave them in the ground for another two weeks.

Storage
Onions can be stored by the string method (*see garlic page 64*), in plastic netting or simply by tying in bundles.

Parsnip

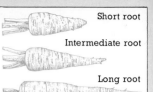

Short root

Intermediate root

Long root

Varieties
Short rooted varieties are suitable for shallow soils, but long and intermediate varieties need deep, fertile soil.

Site	sun or a little shade
Soil	moist, deep, stone-free
Soil preparation	single-dig if short-rooted types to be grown, double-dig if long kinds, in late autumn–early winter, and use site manured for previous crop; rake in general compound fertilizer a week or so before sowing
Sow	early–mid spring; station sow 1·2cm($\frac{1}{2}$in) deep, 10–20cm(4–8in) apart, depending on root length, in rows 30cm(1ft) apart; germination time 21–28 days
Thin	to leave strongest seedling at each station when this can be seen
Water	generously in dry weather
Harvest	when leaves begin to yellow in autumn; can be left in ground through winter, but mark rows; mice/rats may eat them in ground
Store	dig up in early winter, clean soil off roots and remove any leaves, put in layers in boxes of dry sand or peat in dry, frostproof place
Troubles	canker, occasionally celery fly or greenfly in dry weather
Varieties	*short-rooted*, Avonresister, White Gem; *long-rooted*, Improved Hollow Crown, Tender and True

Digging
Single digging is suitable for short rooted types, but long varieties need double digging.

Forked roots
Stony soils will cause roots to divide.

Station sowing
This is a good method of growing parsnips in unsuitable ground. Prepare individual holes at least 60cm (2ft) deep with sifted soil and sow three seeds to each hole. Later, thin to the strongest seedling.

Pepper, sweet

Site	greenhouse or sunny, warm, south-facing wall, sheltered
Soil	rich, moist, well-drained or good potting compost
Soil preparation	single-dig in mid spring and mix in rotted organic matter; rake in a potash-high compound fertilizer at 90g per sq.m (3oz per sq.yd) about a week after planting
Sow	early spring, indoors in warmth, 18–21°C(65–70°F), 2 seeds to a 5cm(2in) pot, 6mm(¼in) deep, in a good seed compost; germination time 7–14 days
Thin	remove weakest seedling
Pot	put into 7cm(3in) pot when roots fill first pot; put into 17cm(7in) pot at same stage
Transplant	if growing outdoors, in late spring with cloche or frame protection; harden off first; space 45cm(1½ft) apart
Stake	supply 75cm(2½ft) stake at planting time for each plant
Feed	liquid-feed from mid summer at weekly intervals with a potash-high fertilizer
Water	keep well supplied with water
Harvest	when 7–12cm(3–5in) long, from late summer to mid autumn; pepper should be firm and well filled out, either green or red

Discouraging pests
Keeping the greenhouse well damped down will help to prevent red spider infestation.

Other troubles
Greenfly, whitefly, grey mould in cool climates

Note
Remove first flowers before setting to encourage a bigger crop. Peppers need a long growing season to do well.

 **Pea**

Site	sunny or slightly shaded, sheltered from wind
Soil	deep, moist, fertile, slightly acid to slightly alkaline
Soil preparation	double-dig in late autumn or early winter, and mix rotted organic matter into the top 23cm(9in); add lime if required a few weeks later; on sandy soils prepare similarly but in late winter; 2 weeks before sowing, rake in 90g per sq.m (3oz per sq.yd) of superphosphate and 30g(1oz) sulphate of potash to same area; water the dressings in if the soil and weather are dry
Sow	outdoors in succession every 3 weeks from mid spring to mid summer; if cold in spring, put cloches over site 2 weeks in advance and keep cloched until well germinated; sow in frames, in containers, late in early spring; sow 5cm(2in) deep, and 5cm(2in) apart in shallow trenches 20cm(8in) wide, with a double staggered row; allow the expected height of the variety between each trench; sow extra seeds to fill gaps; germination time 10–20 days
Transplant	as soon as leaves start to unfold; harden protected seedlings off first
Stake	put in twiggy sticks, canes or strong wire, or plastic-covered netting 0·6–1·5m(2–5ft) tall, when plants are 7cm(3in) high

Sowing
A shallow trench is easy to make in fine soil by drawing the back of the spade through it.

Cloches
Putting cloches over the sowing site for two weeks before sowing will warm the soil. Keep the cloches on until seedlings are established.

Pea

Weed	frequently until well grown
Water	if weather is dry; copiously with tepid water at flowering time, and again when pods have set
Mulch	after watering
Harvest	early summer–early autumn, when pods have filled out completely, about 3 weeks after flowering; pick from the base of plant; cut, do not pull, pods; at end of cropping put haulm on compost heap, but leave roots in the soil to supply nitrogen
Troubles	birds attacking seedlings; mice eat seed in soil; pea moth – maggot eats peas in pod, spray 7–10 days after flowering with derris; powdery mildew on late crops
Varieties	*early varieties:* Feltham First, Kelvedon Wonder, Little Marvel, Gullivert (petit pois), Purple-podded; *maincrops:* Onward, Lord Chancellor, Trio
Notes	wrinkle-seeded (marrowfat) peas are better flavoured but much less hardy than round-seeded kinds, which can be sown in warm gardens under cloche in mid–late autumn and early spring

Support
Peas can be satisfactorily supported with twigs and small branches of trees – easy to find in suburban and country areas.

Post and wires

This is perhaps a more convenient method of support for town gardeners to use. Drive posts into the ground and stretch netting between them – supporting it with wires, top and bottom.

Potato

Site	sunny, sheltered from wind
Soil	deep, moist, fertile, slightly heavy
Soil preparation	double-dig in early winter and mix in rotted organic matter; fork in a proprietary potato fertilizer 2 weeks before planting
Sprout	set egg-sized tubers ('seed') to sprout, on end, in a cool, light, but frost-free place in mid winter for early crops, and in late winter for maincrops; cut up large tubers so there are at least 3 'eyes' on each piece
Plant	when sprouts are about 2cm(¾in) long; early varieties in early spring, maincrops in mid spring; plant sprout-end upwards 7cm(3in) deep in heavy soil, 15cm(6in) deep in sandy soil; space early crops 30cm(1ft) apart in rows 60cm(2ft); maincrops 38cm(15in) apart, with 75cm(2½ft) between rows; protect emerging shoots from frost
Earth up	either make ridges 30cm(1ft) high over rows immediately after planting, using soil at sides, or start to earth-up when shoots are about 15cm(6in) tall; draw soil from sides until only the tops of shoots are exposed, repeat 3 weeks later
Weed	frequently until growth well advanced
Water	heavily in dry weather; if short of water at any time, tubers will split after moisture is applied

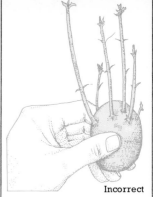

Incorrect

Correct

Seed potatoes
When ready for planting, seed potatoes should be firm, clean and dry. A well sprouted tuber should have at least 3 shoots which should be no more than 2cm (3/4in) long. Reject tubers with shoots that are long and spindly. Tubers with sufficient healthy shoots can be divided so there are about 3 on each segment.

Potato

Planting

Harvest	earlies in early–mid summer, 13 weeks after planting; 2nd earlies in late summer, 6 weeks later, and maincrops early–mid autumn, 20–22 weeks after planting; dig up first earlies as wanted, they will keep a few weeks; leave 2nd earlies and maincrop tubers to dry in sun for a few hours; tops (haulm) of earlies will still be green when they are ready for digging, maincrops will have withered
Store	clean 2nd earlies and maincrops of soil; dry and store in bags or boxes in complete darkness in a mice- and frostproof place; 2nd earlies start to sprout after early winter; also store in clamp outdoors: heap into a mound, cover with straw 10cm(4in) thick and a thin layer of soil, leave for a few days, then add further soil to make layer 15cm(6in) thick, dug out so as to form channel round base of mound; leave tufts of straw poking through soil
Troubles	potato blight, black leg (base of potato stem turns black), dig up and discard; wireworm, slugs, scab, Colorado beetle (orange and black-striped small beetle which eats holes in leaves) – report to local government authorities
Varieties	*early*, Arran Pilot, Epicure, Duke of York; *2nd early*, Maris Peer, Red Craig's Royal; *maincrop*, Majestic, King Edward, Desiree, Pentland Crown, Golden Wonder
Notes	line planting holes or trenches with grass cuttings to cut down superficial scab

Plant in v-shaped trenches and set tubers 30cm (1ft) or 38cm (15in) apart, depending on type (*see opposite*).

Earthing up
Draw soil up around the shoots as they appear. This protects them from frost and later shields the new tubers from light – which makes them green and poisonous.

 # Radish

Site	sunny or slightly shaded
Soil	moist, fertile, neutral to slightly alkaline
Soil preparation	single-dig in late autumn–early winter and mix in rotted organic matter for spring and early summer sowings; single-dig shortly before sowing where they are to follow another crop in summer or autumn; add lime if required several weeks after organic matter; rake in bone-meal at 90g per sq.m (3oz per sq.yd) a few days before sowing; soil should be very crumbly on surface, but firm beneath
Sow	summer varieties outdoors every 2 weeks from late in early spring until late summer, in rows 15cm(6in) apart – in shade for summer crops; winter varieties, outdoors in mid or late summer in rows 30cm(1ft) apart; sow all thinly 6mm(¼in) deep; germination time 4–10 days
Thin	summer varieties to 5cm(2in) apart immediately they are large enough to handle; winter varieties to 10cm(4in) apart
Water	copiously in dry weather
Harvest	summer varieties from late spring–mid autumn, 21–42 days after sowing, depending on time of sowing; winter kinds from mid autumn, can be left in ground all winter

Recommended varieties

summer types

Saxerre

Sparkler

Cherry Belle

Winter types

Black Spanish Round

Black Spanish long

China Rose

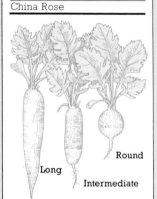

Round

Long

Intermediate

Radish types

Radishes come in 3 different shapes and can be red, white or black. Winter radishes can weigh up to ½kg (1lb) each, and be 30cm (1ft) long.

Storage/troubles

Dig up roots in early winter, clean off soil and remove the tops. Store in layers of dry peat in a dark, frostproof place. Flea beetle is the only serious pest. Club root sometimes attacks.

Shallot

Site	sunny
Soil	light, well-drained
Soil preparation	single-dig in late autumn–early winter and mix in rotted organic matter if not being grown on site manured for previous crop; firm soil by treading just before planting, and rake surface
Plant	sets in late winter–early spring; space 15cm(6in) apart, in rows 23cm(9in) apart; cover half the bulb when planting; put the sets on the soil, do not push them into it; use bulbs 3cm(¾in) in diameter; cut off withered leaves before planting, otherwise birds will pull them out of the ground; shoots appear 1–3 weeks later
Weed	frequently until well established
Train	cut off flowering stems if they appear
Harvest	mid–late summer, when tops begin to yellow, about 18 weeks after planting; dig up, clean and put to dry in a shady place outdoors for a few days, or indoors in warmth; one bulb should produce 5–6 large, or 8–10 small, new ones
Store	hang in bunches by withered leaves in a dry, dark, frostproof place
Varieties	Giant Long-keeping Red, Giant Long-keeping Yellow

Firm plot and rake

Soil preparation
Shallots need plenty of rotted organic matter and a good fine soil which should be firmed and raked before planting.

Note
Birds pull newly planted sets out of the soil – often in spite of protection – examine daily and replant until firmly established. Buy sets from reputable seedsmen to reduce the risk of virus.

Spinach

Site	sun or some shade
Soil	moist, heavy, fertile, neutral – slightly alkaline for spinach beet
Soil preparation	for summer crops single-dig in late autumn–early winter and mix in rotted organic matter; add lime if required a few weeks later; for winter crops single-dig ground manured for previous crop
Sow	round-seeded *summer spinach* from early spring–mid summer; prickly-seeded *winter spinach* late summer–early autumn; *spinach beet* mid spring and mid summer; *Swiss Chard* late spring and mid summer; sow spinach and spinach beet 2·5cm(1in) deep, Swiss Chard 1·2cm($\frac{1}{2}$in) deep; sow spinach very thinly in rows 30cm(1ft) apart; station sow spinach beet and Swiss Chard 15cm(6in) apart in rows 45cm(1$\frac{1}{2}$ft) apart; germination time 10–24 days
Thin	*spinach* to 10cm(4in) and then to 20cm(8in) apart; *spinach beet* and *Swiss Chard* to the strongest at each station and then remove alternate plants leaving 30cm(1ft) between remainder
Weed	frequently in early stages
Water	heavily during dry weather, otherwise summer spinach, in particular, runs to flower

Spinach types

Summer

Winter
New Zealand

Spinach beet

Prickly seeded winter varieties will provide crops in autumn and spring. New Zealand spinach will tolerate dry climates. Spinach beet – a kind of beetroot – will stand the winter.

Spinach

Mulch	if soil light and sandy
Protect	winter crops with cloches
Harvest	summer crops late spring–early autumn, about 8 weeks from sowing; winter crops late autumn–mid spring, 14 weeks from sowing; take outside leaves first and pick only a few from each plant; thinnings can be used; stems of Swiss Chard can also be eaten, cooked like asparagus
Troubles	slugs on seedlings and young plants; occasionally greenfly in dry weather; birds in winter
Varieties	*spinach:* Long-standing Round, Broad-leaved Prickly; *Perpetual Spinach* (spinach beet): Silver Chard and Ruby Chard (seakale beet)
Notes	New Zealand spinach is a kind which will stand hot, dry weather without bolting; it is a trailing spreading plant with succulent leaves, not hardy, which needs 90cm(3ft) space all round; sow in late spring, and harvest by removing tips of shoots as well as leaves; allow an average of 5 spinach plants per person to obtain sufficient crop at any one picking (slightly less for the other kinds)

Watering
Summer spinach will run to flower very quickly if not kept well supplied with water. This is especially important when the plants are young.

Harvesting
Cut the outside leaves from each plant as they are ready and keep repeating this process throughout the growing season. Perpetual spinach has an exceptionally long season.

Swede

Site	sunny
Soil	moist, slightly heavy, fertile, slightly alkaline
Soil preparation	single-dig in late autumn–early winter, and grow on a site manured for a previous crop; add lime if required a few weeks later; rake in a compound fertilizer comparatively low in nitrogen content about 2 weeks before sowing
Sow	outdoors in late spring–early summer; sow seed thinly 2cm(¾in) deep in rows 45cm(1½ft) apart; germination time 6–10 days
Thin	at 3-leaf stage and again to a final spacing of 25cm(10in)
Water	well in dry weather
Mulch	if soil is light, after final thinning
Harvest	mid autumn, 20–24 weeks after sowing, or when roots are 7–17cm(3–7in) diameter
Store	clean off soil, top and tail the roots, and put them in layers in dry peat or sand; use boxes; put in cool but frostproof, dark place
Troubles	flea beetle, slugs and snails, club-root, occasionally greenfly in dry weather
Varieties	Western Perfection (purple top) for summer crops, Mancunian, Best of All for maincrops and storage

The Swede
Swedes are members of the turnip family, but they are hardier and sweeter. It is possible to leave them in the soil throughout winter – so they do not present a storage problem.

Mulching
Swedes should be mulched after the final thinning.

Sweetcorn

Site	sunny, sheltered from strong wind
Soil	light to medium, fertile
Soil preparation	single-dig heavy soil in late autumn–early winter and mix in rotted organic matter if not manured for a previous crop; double-dig light soil in early spring and mix in rotted organic matter; rake in potash-high compound fertilizer 2 weeks before planting
Sow	indoors in mid spring in warmth, 16°C(60°F); use good seed compost and sow 2 seeds 6mm(¼in) deep in 7cm(3in) peat pots; germination time 6–12 days
Thin	to strongest seedling in each pot
Plant	late spring after hardening off and protect until frost risk past; plant pot and sweetcorn; space 40cm(16in) apart, with 75cm(2½ft) between rows; plant in square or rectangular blocks
Weed	frequently when young
Feed	liquid-feed from flowering time to harvest with potash-high fertilizer if not applied before planting
Water	keep well watered when young
Mulch	when roots appear on surface
Varieties	First of All, Earliking

Sowing/planting
Sweetcorn does not like its roots disturbed – it is best to sow it in fibre pots or peat blocks and transfer them to the open ground when seedlings are big enough.

Harvest
15–18 weeks after sowing when silks are dark brown and damp. Kernels should be milky when pressed.

Note
Pollination is better if plants are grown in blocks rather than rows. Frit fly sometimes attacks tips – apply HCH (g-BHC).

Tomato, indoor

Site	unheated greenhouse
Soil	deep, moist, well-drained, fertile, slightly acid to slightly alkaline, or a good potting compost
Soil preparation	fork over in late autumn–early winter, add lime if required, flood to a depth of 50cm(20in) in 2 or 3 stages; double-dig in late winter and mix in rotted organic matter; fork in a proprietary tomato fertilizer 2 weeks before planting
Sow	at the beginning of spring, in warmth, 16–18°C(60–65°F); sow 2 seeds in each of 5cm(2in) pots and seed compost; germination time 8–11 days
Thin	remove weakest seedlings when obvious
Pot	put into 7cm(3in) pots of good potting compost when small pot filled with roots
Plant	in greenhouse in mid spring when plants are 12–17cm(5–7in) tall; plant 45cm × 75cm (1½ × 2ft) apart; water the planting hole but do not water the plants in after planting.
Water	water well every few days in early stages, from 7–10 days after planting; when fruit begins to set, give each plant 4·5l(1gal) tepid water every other day, and water more frequently in hot weather
Mulch	in mid summer with moist peat or rotted organic matter

Planting
Knock plants out of their pots, keeping the root ball intact. Loosen the soil around the root tips just before planting.

Feeding
Liquid feed with a potash-high fertiliser when fruit on the first truss is marble sized. In late summer, change to a nitrogen-high fertiliser and use regularly.

Tomato, indoor

Harvest	mid summer–mid autumn, from lowest fruit cluster upwards; pick with part of stalk attached, breaking off at 'knuckle'
Store	last fruits can be picked pale green and put in dark, warm place to colour
Troubles	*tomato leaf-mould:* brown spots and patches on undersurface of leaves, leaves and plants may die; treatment: remove worst affected leaves, spray remainder with benomyl systemic fungicide; *tomato wilt:* infects from soil through roots, leaves wilt, turn yellow from base upwards; destroy infected plants including roots, sterilize soil or use new soil; *magnesium deficiency:* yellow leaves between main veins, spray leaves 5 times at 2 week intervals with Epsom Salts solution [60g in 4·5l(2oz in 1gal) of water], use less potash in future; *blossom-end rot:* fruit has grey-black sunken patch at one end, keep supplied with sufficient water at all times; *whitefly, red spider mite, tomato moth caterpillar, potato blight, grey mould*
Varieties	Ailsa Craig, Grenadier, Seville Cross, Big Boy
Notes	tomatoes need warmth rather than sun, in which fruit and leaves may be scalded; regular, large supplies of water are vital; spray overhead in mornings when flowering to ensure good, complete pollination; can be grown in 23cm(9in) pots

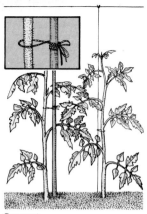

Support
Tomatoes can be tied to individual stakes or trained to grow up wires. Twist the stems clockwise around vertical wires attached to an overhead horizontal wire.

Unusual tomatoes
Very large – perhaps ½kg(1lb) – fruit can be obtained by stopping the plant at the third truss. Alternatively, you could try growing one of the yellow, striped or plum-shaped varieties.

Tomato, outdoor

Site	sunny, warm, sheltered, against south or west facing wall
Soil	as indoor tomatoes
Soil preparation	double-dig late winter–early spring and mix in rotted organic matter; add lime a few weeks later if required; rake in tomato fertilizer 2 weeks before planting
Sow	indoors mid spring in 16–18°C(60–65°F) as indoor types
Thin	as indoor types
Pot	as indoor types
Plant	outdoors at end of late spring or in early summer (as indoor types) protect from cold until established; *space* 45 × 60cm(1½ × 2ft) for cordons, 60 × 75cm(2 × 2½ft) for bush tomatoes
Feed	as indoor types
Water	frequently and heavily in dry weather
Harvest	as indoor types, but start late in summer
Store	as indoor types
Troubles	as indoor types
Varieties	Outdoor Girl, Gardener's Delight, Sigmabush, Roma

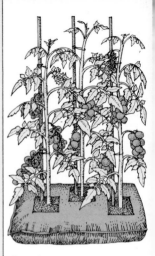

Grow bags
These bags, which can be bought from any garden supplier, contain a perfectly balanced soil for growing tomatoes. They are ideal for balconies, patios etc. – some people even use them in greenhouses.

Ripening tomatoes
At the end of the season, but before the danger of frost, bring the unripe fruit indoors and ripen them on a sunny window ledge. Alternatively, lay the plants down on a bed of clean straw and cover them with cloches.

Turnip

Site	sunny, shelter from cold wind for early sowings
Soil	moist, fertile, light, slightly alkaline, largely free of stones
Soil preparation	single-dig in late autumn–early winter; use a site manured for a previous crop; add lime if required a few weeks later; rake in bonemeal at 90g per sq.m (3oz per sq.yd) a month before sowing
Sow	early–mid spring for immediate use, cloche early spring sowing; mid–late summer for maincrops and storing; sow thinly 1·2cm(½in) deep in rows 23–30cm(9–12in) apart; germination time 6–12 days
Thin	early crops to 15cm(6in) apart; maincrops 30cm(1ft) apart; thin immediately seedlings are large enough to handle, otherwise they do not grow good roots
Water	keep well supplied with water in dry weather
Harvest	early crops late spring–early summer, 8–9 weeks after sowing, when 3–6cm(1¼–2½in) diameter; maincrops early–late autumn 10–12 weeks after sowing 7–10cm(3–4in) diameter for best flavour; can be left in ground all winter
Store	dig up in early winter, clean, remove any foliage, and store in layers in dry peat or sand in mice-proof boxes and a dark, frostproof place

Recommended varieties

Early
Snowball
Milan White
Maincrop
Golden Ball
Manchester Market (*Green Top stone*)

Flat

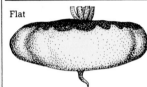

Long

Globe

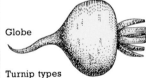

Turnip types
There are no particular advantages to any one shape, but the maincrop varieties are usually round.

Troubles
Flea beetle, slugs, club root, cabbage root fly.

Note
Keep growing fast, for tender, well-flavoured roots; use them within a day or two of lifting.

Vegetable marrow

Site	sunny, sheltered
Soil	rich, moist, deep
Soil preparation	for each plant, dig a hole 38cm(15in) deep and 75cm(2½ft) square, and mix rotted organic matter with soil to be returned in a 1:1 ratio; prepare in mid spring; space the holes 120cm(4ft) apart for bush marrows, 180cm(6ft) apart for trailing kinds
Sow	indoors in mid spring in warmth, 16–18°C(60–65°F); sow 2 seeds in a 7cm(3in) pot of good potting compost; germination time 3–8 days
Thin	remove weakest seedling in each pot
Pot	into 11cm(4½in) pot when the first pot is filled with roots
Plant	harden off and plant outdoors at the end of late spring–early summer; protect from cold
Water	heavily in dry weather
Mulch	on light soils, halfway through summer
Harvest	courgettes 12–14 weeks after sowing, when 7–10cm(3–4in) long, mid summer onwards; marrows 14–16 weeks after sowing, when 20–25cm(8–10in) long, late summer–mid autumn
Store	cut on a dry day in mid autumn, hang in nets in cool, dark place

Recommended varieties

bush type

Improved Green Bush

Smallpak

Golden Zuchini

Trailing type

Long Green Striped

Vegetable Spaghetti (*trailing*)

Little Gem (*round*)

Custard Yellow (*squash*)

Pumpkin

Squash

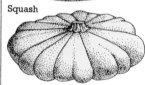

Marrow types
Marrows, squashes and pumpkins are all varieties of the same species. The flat squashes are usually grown for summer use; pumpkin varieties can be stored for quite long periods.

Troubles
Slugs on young plants; mildew, grey mould – remove blossom after fruit sets; collar rot (stem rots at soil level) destroy badly affected plants.

Glossary of terms

Blanch
To exclude light from the foliage of a plant, thus preventing it from turning green.

Blind
A plant which cannot produce flowering growth is said to be 'blind'.

Bolting
Running to flower before plants have matured. Usually due to hot, dry conditions.

Catch crop
A quick maturing crop, planted on ground prepared for a later-sown vegetable.

Drill
A groove made in the soil, usually up to 5cm(2in) in depth, into which seeds will be sown.

Earthing up
Drawing the soil around the stem of a plant to provide protection, or to blanch the stems.

Haulm
A word used to refer to the foliage of peas, beans and, sometimes, potatoes.

Hardening off
The gradual introduction of outdoor conditions of plants raised in warmth.

Intercropping
Growing quick maturing plants between rows of other vegetables i.e., lettuce between rows of broad beans.

Legume
A plant which produces pods.

Mulch
Anything which is placed on the soil to retain moisture or warmth. A mulch may also be used to keep down weeds.

Overwinter
Quite simply, keeping a plant from autumn through to spring. Some plants have to be put into warmth, most would need to be under glass.

Set(s)
1. A fruit, eg tomato, which has begun to swell is said to be 'set'.
2. The seed bulbs of onions and shallots are called sets.

Station sowing
Sowing in separately prepared holes, rather than in drills.

Succession sowing
Sowing seeds of one crop at intervals of a few days or weeks. The idea is to provide a continuous supply of the crop.

Spit
The depth of a garden spade or fork.

Tilth
A fine crumbly soil, suitable for sowing. Derived from the word 'till'.

Trickle Irrigation
A method of providing a continuous supply of water for plants such as watercress.

Keep your own records

VEGETABLE	SOW/PLANT – DATES	HARVEST – DATES	NOTES

VEGETABLE	SOW/PLANT – DATES	HARVEST – DATES	NOTES

Plot planner

Use the squared grid, opposite, or make one of your own on graph paper, to mark out the plots in your garden. You can use it to plan your crop rotation system and to keep a record of the precise location of plants sown, planted or transplanted. Enter notes about applications of fertilizers, weedkillers etc. and you will have a complete dossier on your vegetable growing activities.

Use the chart on pages 90/91 to enter the dates of sowings, plantings etc., so that you can keep a log of the progress of the crops in your garden.

Index

In the following index, figures in italics refer to illustrations, those in bold to the pages of growing instructions.

Acknowledgments

The 'How To' Book of
Vegetable Gardening was
created by Simon Jennings
and Company Limited.
We are grateful to the
following individuals
and organisations for
their assistance in the
making of this book:

Pat Brindley: *photograph, page 6*
John Couzins: *cover and title page photographs*
The Dover Archive: *engravings and embellishments*
Richard Lewis: *line and tone illustrations*
Robert Micklewright: *line illustrations*
Susan Milne: *colour illustrations*
Anna Pavord: *compilation of index*
Christopher Perry: *additional artwork*
Michael Woods: *colour illustration*
Helena Zakrsewska – Rucinska: *hand tinting of engravings*

Typesetting by Servis Filmsetting Ltd., Manchester
Headline setting by Facet Photosetting, London

Special thanks to Norman Ruffell and
the staff of Swaingrove Ltd., Bury St. Edmunds,
Suffolk, for the lithographic reproduction.

'HOW TO'